A Warm Mirror Neuron on a Memory

An Avant-garde Book of Modern Poetry

by
E. E. E.

Also by E. E. E.

NON-FICTION
The Marxist Analysis of Immigration
Game Theory: Everyday Applications
Schema: Religio Proto-Indo-European *Est Ab Origine*

NOVELLA (*récit*)
T.H.B.

SHORT FICTION
A Collection of Short Stories

POETRY | *DICHTUNG*
A Warm Mirror Neuron on a Memory

CRITICISM
A Collection of Criticisms

LETTER
A Collection of Letters

GRAPHIC NOVEL
T.H.B.: A Graphic Novel

MULTIMEDIA
x.com/programmabiliti
YouTube.com/programmabilities
NotebookLM.Google.com/notebook/ba2b51c3-1a55-4a79-8a90-0493207aa8ca/audio

Published by Programmabilities

A Warm Mirror Neuron on a Memory™

An Avant-garde Book of Modern Poetry

von

E. E. E.

A *Programmabilities* Book
"Get with the program!"®

Luxemburg • *Kraków*

Published by Programmabilities®

Copyright © 2025, Programmabilities.com

A CIP catalogue record for this book is available from the British Library.

1 3 5 7 9 10 8 6 4 2 0

ISBN: 978-1-7326264-2-3 (electronic)
ISBN: 978-0-615-56694-8 (paper)
ASIN: B00GQFT6QM
LCC: JA71-80
BISAC: POL070000   POLITICAL SCIENCE / Public Policy / Immigration
LCCN: 2014903401
OCLC: 000000000
Publisher ID: 7326264

First Programmabilities Edition

Programmabilities is an imprint of Programmabilities.com

programmabilities

A Programmabilities Book
"Get with the program!"®

This leaf intentionally left blank

Dedication

To the real primate,
who lives within us all.

Ouroboros

Epigraph

"To be, or not to be [identity], that is the *question*:
Whether 'tis nobler in the mind to suffer
The slings and arrows of outrageous fortune,
Or to take Arms against a Sea of troubles,
And by opposing end them: "

—*Hamlet*

"The enemy is our own *question* as a figure [identity]
And he will hunt us, as we will him to the same end."[1]

—Theodor Däubler, "Sang an Palermo"

All being is premised by *negation*. We define by negation. Exclusion is a necessary premise of inclusion. Negation both separates and connects.

—para. Hegel

YouTube.com/watch?v=6eWkAOiPk6q[2]

---

[1] Carl Schmitt quotes this verse in "Wisdom from the Cell". And Heinrich Meiers' Schmitt book says: "In epigrammatic sharpness this poetic phrase seems to give expression to the insight that the political serves self-knowledge and arises from self-knowledge. ...read it as follows: We know ourselves insofar as we know our enemy and insofar as we define our enemy by defining ourselves. *We know him to be our enemy who places us in question* or the one whom we place in question insofar as we 'know' ourselves, as we make ourselves known to ourselves and to others. The enemy proves to be our friend against his will on the way to self-knowledge, and our self-knowledge is transformed suddenly into a source of enmity when it assumes a visible figure."

[2] Leibniz said, from one unity number all numbers are created. "...the mystic elegance of the binary system...made Leibniz exclaim: *Omnibus ex nihil ducendis sufficit unum.* (One suffices to derive all out of nothing.) ...Leibniz saw in his binary arithmetic the image of Creation ...He imagined that Unity represented God, and Zero the void; that the Supreme Being drew all beings from the void, just as unity and zero express all numbers in his system of numeration." —*Number*

"All creatures derive from God and from nothingness. Their self-being is of God, their nonbeing is of nothing. Numbers too show this..., and the essences of things are like numbers. No creature can be without nonbeing; otherwise it would be God... The only self-knowledge is to distinguish well between our self-being and our nonbeing... Within our selfbeing there lies an infinity, a footprint or reflection of the omniscience and omnipresence of God." —Leibniz

Table of Contents (TOC) | *Inhalt*

Author's Note

Note: This book is "Turing complete"—it mainly uses the central theme of the old jargon of Marxism, *but* it could have mainly used the jargon of any other coding system (to say the same thing), such as game theory, free-markets libertarianism, conservatism, humanitarianism, economics, Darwinism, Freudianism, Hinduism, Abrahamism, civil rights, primatology, empiricism, progressivism, *etc*. And, as so-called Critical Theory says, "Every theory [application] is a response to an interest that the theory [applicant] has."

Foreword | *Vorwort*

"What is here, is found elsewhere
What is not here, is nowhere!"
—foreword to *Mahabharata* (*Bhagavad Gita*)

"This book is dynamite! Go online and buy it now!"
—Jon Doe PhD, professor of Political Science, Krakow University

The communist Fabian Society logo, founders of the free-market capitalism London School of Economics

Preface | *Vorwort*

"Freedom is the freedom to say that *two plus two* make *four*. [A=A. —The law of identity.] If that is granted, all else follows." [3] (George Orwell, *1984*)

"In the end the Party would announce that *two and two* made *five* [a normative 'consensus norm'—rendering impossible *two plus two* make *four,* identity], and you have to believe it. It was inevitable that they should make that claim sooner or later: the logic of their position demanded it. Not merely the validity of experience, but the very existence of external reality, was tacitly denied by their philosophy. The heresy of heresies was common sense." (Orwell, *1984,* Where "Thought Police", the instrument used to enforce their élites' will and ideology, punish "thought-crimes" against their "doublethink".)

"Fires will be kindled to testify that two and two make four. Swords will be drawn to prove that leaves are green in summer." (Chesterson)

"The revolution will be complete when the language is perfect." (Orwell, *1984*)

CAN THE MEDIA control the *cortex*? Who controls the media (where the primary concern of the establishment media, the "fourth estate," is norm-policing the public, not informing them)? Has the élites' doctrine of Liberalism created today's displacement of native Europeans? The cultural norm of Liberal extremism has driven the natives into an endangered-species in places such as the emirates of England, France, Belgium, Germany, and Sweden (where, statistically *per capita*, there has been a 6-9 average IQ[4] point drop in the past two decades). Authoritarian Liberal extremism is evidently the issue—that has reached hegemonic consensus amongst the native extant west Europeans *via* the media and the élites who exploit the humanitarian loopholes of liberalism. How can the language of modern Marxism and its particularism and its identitarian warfare in the realm of the *cortex* shed light on the exploitation of liberalism's gross weaknesses (Schmittian denial of the political)?

> The truth is our ruling-class prefers immigrants to [Europeans]. Diversity is their religion. And in their own way, they're religious extremists. When the safety and well-being of [Europeans] conflicts with their faith, they will choose their faith every time. (Tucker Carlson)

These questions posed themselves to me with a particular-criticality as I toured England, just another Brown economic-zone of Europe, where, as Enoch Powell predicted, "the black man [has] the whip hand over the white man," (but what does "white" mean says the "no-sides" liberal), and saw the Englishmen were all liberal extremists mouthing the same platitudes from the free-market capitalist-liberal far-left élites. —A "camp of the saints." Where young aboriginal Englænder quickly jump to defend and backup their colonisers (called "black heads" in Russian-speaking lands), the African-identitarians and Muslim-identitarians who swamp their cities and breed out their women ovum (Muslim men in Europe have a *motto* amongst themselves, they "only want girls who are unmixed," who

---

[3] But, Bertrand Russel pointed out that in a closed formal system, 2+2 can equal 5. —Just set 2 equal to 2.5. (para.)
[4] Ironically, IQ tests were initially championed by the Left when meritocracy meant helping the victims of aristocracy. But now the Left denies science concerning biological differences betwixt folk.

are "white" because "white means clean." —"Mixture is predicated on purity."), from the smallest criticisms, in a *dhimmitude*[5] (Stockholm Syndrome) dynamic. *Jihad* takes place through "immigration" to "the house of war" (non-Muslim countries) or "house of the West" in later Ottoman sources. Islam, meaning *surrender*, is a political ideology. Talk to a Frenchman, Dutchman, Englishman and they are almost all the same; they have surrendered in their hearts. They have surrendered politically to Islam and colonisation by Africans (Sub-Saharan African and North-African). —To a multicultural/non-European future. *They do not remember that things had once been different.* Islam now being a synonym for *multikulti*. Europeans are already *Dhimi* in their own homelands. England or "Cuck Island", now, "a country of immigrants," is no longer an English country. Such is the pitiful *case* with European men who have been BBC'd (double-*entendre* intended) their whole lives; where historical/cultural de-Europeanisation is

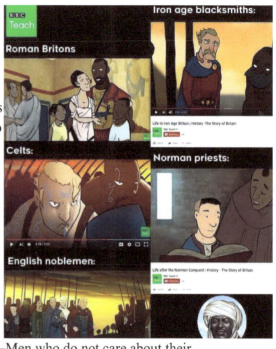

state policy in the "Transition to Black Rule." —Men who do not care about their identity—men who got lost. While, as a result, everywhere these indoctrinated Englishmen living under occupation had been squeezed out of their own homelands by more and more and evermore non-European identitarian settlers. —Much like I saw in Palestine under "The Occupation"; where world Jewry, those who wrote the genocidal Torah c*oda* that legitimises Israel, brings *tikkun olam* to the anti-Semitic[6] Palestinians. And I could see clearly that it was *not* something forecasted for the future. —It was an accomplished fact-on-the-ground[7]. The "phase transition"[8] has already happened. ("Polish Experts: 'Europe is at The End of its Existence. Western Europe is Practically Dead'") England *was* a state of "strange death" (*blancocide*), in the words of the gay Douglas Murray. —Or, "It's finished", in the words of scientist Richard Lynn. And clearly with the strange death of native west Europeans in their territories there was no coming back to life again. . . . So, now, in the *nakba* of the occupied west bank Europe, which way hither and yon? And how?

So, like Foucault, I engaged in my own little "archeology" of the Liberal programme (which led to the Marxian hackers who hacked it for exploits). This archaeology pointed to the *somewhat* importance of the Frankfurt School of *Marxismus* in influencing liberalism to the ends (interests) that its *particular* practitioners wanted. So I investigated "what worked" (Marxism). (And I discovered that modern Marxism just meant dialectics in theory and "identity-politics"—also called "identitarian politics"—in practice.). —"What won" and "who won." As how a slave studies his conqueror and learns his *modus operandi*.

---

[5] wikipedia.org/wiki/*Bat_Ye'or*
[6] the "fascist", "hateful", "virulent", "toxic", "pathological disease of the mind"
[7] wikipedia.org/wiki/Facts_on_the_ground
[8] mathworld.wolfram.com/PhaseTransition.html

"He who controls the present, controls the past. He who controls the past, controls the future." (Orwell)

Europeans are conquered folks. —They cannot say "no" (Hegel's slave-consciousness cannot *negate*). How did the European's élite become "the Judas"? And how can the devastated autochthonous Europeans win emancipation/differentiation from the non-European colonists and from the hostile élite's *cortex*-hegemony and drive them both out? How long will gullible Europeans cuckold[9] for the hostile élite and the non-European colonists, who suppress their fertility, plunder European social-services/jobs/wages/housing/ovum, indoctrinate European kids in mass media, and bankrupting replacement-immigration?

Marxism being particularistic/identitarian is the opposite of "dumb terminal" universalistic/humanitarian Liberalism. Neo-Marxism, Critical Theory, dialectics, particularism, identitarianism (identity-politics), norming, and the propagandistic media have a proven track-record of success in exploiting *cortices*. The Schmittian "enemies" of aboriginal Europeans used it to destroy and colonise the liberal west Europe aborigines. And aboriginal Europeans can shed their gross illiteracy and use it a bit too to, maybe, avoid their, monotonically increasing[10], complete(d) genocide.

"They have been trained like monkeys to beg for their own dispossession and genocide." (Frank Raymond)

In the news one liberal leader's refutation of the charge of *blancocide*, which has now become a *mantra* slogan for the left-posing anti-Europeans, was, quote, "*It's satisfying to always remember that none of the descendents* [*sic*] *of the people screaming about the* myth *of white-genocide will be white.*"

> That scorn of a people of other races, the knowledge that one's own is best, the triumphant joy at feeling oneself to be part of humanity's finest—none of that had ever filled these youngsters' addled brains, or at least so little that the monstrous cancer implanted in the Western conscience had quashed it in no time at all. (Jean Raspail, *Camp of the Saints, 1973*) ∎

Herr E. E. E. von Luxemburg
9 September 2025

---

[9] "Each year, the Huns [Avars] came to the Slavs, to spend the winter with them; then they took the wives and daughters of the Slavs and slept with them, and among the other mistreatments [already mentioned] the Slavs were also forced to pay levies to the Huns. But the sons of the Huns, who were [then] raised with the wives and daughters of these Wends [Slavs] could not finally endure this oppression anymore and refused obedience to the Huns and began, as already mentioned, a rebellion." —*Chronicle of Fredegar*, circa *642*

[10] mathworld.wolfram.com/MonotoneIncreasing.html

Introduction | *die Einleitung*

> "Words hammer continually at the eyes and ears of America. . . . Knowledge of how to use this enormous amplifying system becomes a matter of primary concern to those who are interested in socially constructive action." —Edward Bernays, *Engineering of Consent*

"I AM not sure why I was chosen," wrote the Jew-identitarian Eve Ensler in her very first sentence troll of her "Introduction" section to *The Vagina Monologues*. —An extremely poor book of no merit which was hailed ("We are *interpellated*, or repeatedly 'hailed' into subject positions," wrote Althusser) to victory (platformed—Old English *sige*, ex. seize, "to hold" meant victory) by the establishment's élites[11] (*élite* is from French *elect* meaning chosen) as one of the most all-time greats of political writing.

As introductions have an eye to the import of first premises (*logoi*), to wit I will appropriate her device for my introduction. —By way of introduction, *I am not sure why I was chosen*, but I decided to hail[12] or interpellate this, somewhat of a *pastiche* as Céline would say, *essai*[13] on the particularistic grammar[14] of identity and the "syntactic structures"[15] (and neural wiring that gives rise to such) of politics.

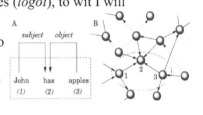

The logic of this language is that, because folks have identities, Achen and Bartels' central claim that "human life is group life" explains much of politics.[16] That will be ever thus.

The fatal flaw with the logic (first premises) of the post-West's liberalism is that, what sealed its folk's doom was that, as Carl Schmitt demonstrated, its "civic" logic denied "the political". Like how well-formed (grammatical) logic can be a *valid* argument even though its false premises/data/grounds make it not a *sound*/grounded argument/warrant. —Unlike (contrary to) the liberalism, with its individualistic based universalism, the Marxist (Hegelian) dialectic, with its particularism—political thinking, identity, Gramscian norming, and group interests—*is* cognizant of this binary validities property of logic (logically valid arguments *versus* logically valid sound/grounded arguments/warrants).

> "[the difference between a master and a slave or dog is that] the slave [dog] does not know what his master is doing;" —*John 15:15.* (aka "[tail] wag the dog") ❙

---

[11] The term *élite* (literally meaning "the chosen," the elect) is a word coined by Vilfredo Pareto.

[12] "hail" was still used for hello in Shakespeare's day. And *good-bye* means god-be-with-ye.

[13] *Aufsatz Versuch*

[14] grammar is hierarchical

[15] Rudolf Carnap saw the task of philosophy as the study of the logical syntax of language, the way in which language, taken as a system of *formulare* for calculation, hangs together.

[16] Also, "Kinder and Kalmoe argue that political behaviour is driven by group identity dynamics." "Normal people are instinct-driven rationalizers motivated by group loyalty dynamics, not ideologies."

Quotation 1

"All those moments will be lost in time, like tears in rain." —*Blade Runner*

"...nothing should ever be done that should be done. It has to come out like a good hot beer shit. A good hot beer shit is glorious man, you get up, you turn around, you look at it, you're proud, the fumes, the stink of the turds, you look at it, you say God I did it, I'm good. Then you flush it away. Then there's that sense of sadness, and just the water is there. It's like writing a good poem. You just do it. It's a beer shit. It's nothing to analyse. There's nothing to say. It's just done. Got it..." —Bukowski, *poetry is a hot beer shit*

"However, the uterus of my mental world has received a tremendous ejaculation of the sperm from Friedrich Nietzsche, so that I feel like a bitch with a full belly. He's the man for me!" —Strindberg

Gracile

Poem 1   *2011/10*. Audio: YouTube.com/watch?v=0Y-eCqsmnLQ

A Warm Mirror Neuron on a Memory

In the moment there was an emotion.

Little or[17] deep—there was a moment.

When there was a feeling.

Brief or lengthy—there was a feeling.

And I saw it. On your face.

On your face ; I saw it.

And I received it.

And I will have it—that moment.

That flash.

Of your emotion. On your face.

I have that emotion. Your deep feeling.

For the rest of my days alive.

How little it was—how brief it was.

Still I have it ; treasure it.

A warm mirror neuron on a memory.

For my ever after.

...And regret. To give it back[18] away.

Over my forever.

That I succeeded to fail to keep it—your succumb.

That I prevailed[19] to lose it.

As was must.

> "In, the twilight glow, I see her
> Blue eyes, cryin', in the rain
> And when we kissed goodbye and parted
> I knew that we'd never meet again
>
> Love is like a dyin' ember
> And only memories remain
> and through the ages I'll remember
> Blue eyes, cryin', in the rain"   —Fred Rose

---

[17] logical connective: *and, or, not*

[18] A dative. [& "the term *dative* is grammatically similar to the Sanskrit word *datta*. *Datta* means 'gift' or 'the act of giving'."]

[19] to win

Quotation 2

"No one can be happy who has been thrust outside the pale of truth. And there are two ways that one can be removed from this realm: by lying, or by being lied to." —Seneca

"word following word, I found me words,
deed following deed, I wrought deeds." —*Hávamál*

"The countenance is the portrait of the soul," Cicero said, "and the eyes mark its intentions."

Thought

Poem 2 *2011/10.*
Skull Watch

"Webster … saw the skull beneath the skin." —T.S. Eliot

I see the talking skulls are the people in our lives soon to be dead.

I see the orbital bone[20] of the eye where the white bone will shine when the spirit dies.

Skulls feeling the shame of being so stupid from falling for lies and scams of the other skulls.

Skulls aching the regret of wasting time and money for being so stupid and ignorant and fooled.

Skulls hungering for justice and righteousness.

Not finding it, so some skull doing it, and being the only Fool.

Skulls kissing and mating.

Skulls counting in superior satisfaction from getting over on other skulls.

And skulls counting in growls from being defected[21] on by other skulls.

Yes, counting skulls ; and groups of counting skulls.

Younger skulls are harder to see ; the youthful flesh conceals it best.

I watch the talking skulls and I look at the skull bones.

Where the rotten white bone will reveal when the flesh and spirit dies.

Erectus Walks Amongst Us, Richard D. Fuerletus

---

[20] In anatomy, the **orbital bone** is the cavity or socket of the skull in which the eye & its appendages are situated.

[21] "Defectors" is the main issue of Game Theory.

Quotation 3

"I am a mirage that perceives itself." —Hofstadter, *Godel, Escher, Bach*

"You can't say A is made of B; or *vice versa*.
All mass is interaction." —Feynman
"atoms with consciousness
Here it is standing: atoms with consciousness; matter with curiosity.
Stands at the sea, wondering: I... a universe of atoms
an atom in the universe." —*ibid.*

Down

Poem 3   *2010/11.*
That Figment
Counterfactually, what if you woke-up one day (or blacked-out one day),
Looked into the bathroom's looking-glass,
Opened a panel on the side of your head and, lo, saw that you were a robot—full of wires and metal and plastic circuit-chips?
Would you be heartbroken ; would you cry?
I tell you,
It would be the ultimate horror and tragedy—shock and surprise.
...That you,
That person that you wake-up to every day.
That you,
That guy that you wake-up into being every day.
That story and memory, built up into a house,
At-home-with.
That figment.[22]
That you, that you think that you are, that person-hood.
—Him and his life's story—the aspirations and travails—the *chasing after False idols*[23] and desires. (Seeing the near-death-experience "life review" while flowing down the tunnel tubes.)
Is but a software program written to make it think that a you exists so it more better survives and replicates.
...Not wires and metal and plastic, but, still, it is only a biological computer, a biological machine—dead life—a cold, dry, desert.
Yes, machines can think ...therefore I am.[24]
The ultimate pain, the ultimate torture,
Is not to burn for eternity in hell.
There is a worse notion.
The ultimate pain is
To die
And then
See
The fact that *you* never really existed!
That you were only an icy machine, a computer.
Lo and behold, out in black outer-space you see within a dead cold computer room full of computers—Konrad Zuse's *Rechnender Raum*[25]—just nothing but "calculating space", just

---

[22] figment: Something made up or contrived. A construction.
[23] *Torah* reference.
[24] Descartes' quotation, "I think therefore I am."
[25] Konrad Zuse was the first to propose that physics is just computation, suggesting that the history of our universe is being computed on, say, a cellular automaton. His "*Rechnender Raum*" (Computing/Calculating Space) started the field of Digital Physics in *1967*. (Cellular *autanama*: neighbouring cells that update their values based on surrounding cells, implementing the spread and creation and annihilation of elementary particles.)

calculating away ; —"the most intense aridity." ("The horror.") "Soul crushing."

You never really existed.

False being.[26]

All that time!

Through all that life-span of aspirations and travails ; and chasing.

...There is no greater sadness,

No bigger heartbreak,

No more beyond-hell pain,

Than to see, that after all this,

That you never existed.

That you were only *the figment of your imagination.*[27]

Oh, your body exists, yes.

But your body was not the you that you loved.

What is you, is your innermost self, that person-hood with his strange story.

But that—*that*—that never really existed.

It was only the figment of a machine's[28] imagination.

Some neural software and recursive functions[29]...

That is the greatest tragedy that can be, that can be experienced.

Beyond all that hell was ever said to be.

...and the Father turned his face from the Son.[30] —*That* was the pain of pains.

Non being.[31]

Hell was a cowardly notion for weak fools.

And worse than death is to never have existed.

So I tell you,

The One, the *Brahman* Self, is the only figment of hope that there is.

… "Nagged by confusion, I attempted to orient myself by falling back on a favourite philosopher's ploy. I began naming things. 'Yorick,' I said aloud to my brain, 'you …'"
(lehigh.edu/~mhb0/Dennett-*WhereAmI*.pdf)

"If there were no sun, it would be night." —Heraclitus

"Verily, nothing is dear for its sake; everything (wife, sons, wealth) is dear for the sake of the Self." —*Upanishads*

...And, Zuse thought that the laws of nature should be discrete and not continuous, that difference equations might describe the universe better than differential equations, as Einstein had speculated late in life. Zuse argued correctly that entropy and its growth do not make sense in deterministically computed universes.

[26] False Being: a reference to Martin Buber.

[27] "My existence was beginning to cause me some concern. Was I a mere figment of the imagination?" —Sartre, *Nausea*

[28] 's: wikipedia.org/wiki/Saxon_genitive

[29] "recursive function": a programming action that calls itself; creating a feedback loop. ...& a Cognitive Science model of consciousness. (*I Am A Strange Loop*)

[30] A reference used in Theology to refer to when Jesus cried out upon his death, "My God, my God, why have you forsaken me?" (*Mt. 27:46*).

[31] Negation cognate was the dragon killed by Indra. Or Non-Being: the opposite of being of Paul Tillich.

Quotation 4

"If you do not change direction, you may end up where you are heading." —Lao Tzu

"The more sand that has escaped from the hourglass of our life, the clearer we should see through it." —Sartre

"Now I knew. Everything was exactly as it seemed. And behind it, there was nothing." —*Ibid.*, *Nausea*

"I confused things with their names: that is belief." —*Ibid.*

"My thought is *me*: that's why I can't stop. I exist by what I think." —*Ibid.*

"Poetry is the saga of the unconcealment of what *is*." "Where there is no language there is also no openness of what *is*…" —Heidegger, *Open*

"What's up?"

Poem 4 *2010.* Audio: Soundcloud.com/programmabilities/riding-the-night-train

Riding the Night Train

...I'm getting on the metro[32] subway to-night ;

Howling down the track ;

Looking at the eyes of all the ape-like heads ;

All thinking of their gleaning[33] and their losing.

   Warring, warring, warring.

I'm getting off the subway to-night ;

Screeching to[34] a brake ;

Looking out the eyes of my ape-like head ;

Thinking of my gleaning and my losing.

   Walking, walking, walking.

I'm walking home in the dark ;

Gripped, so I halt ;

And view up at the homeless stars ;

For a moment, I see it's all really nothing.

   Naught, naught, naught.

Then I march on, walking home in the dark ;

The cold, clear, *nocht* air is slipping into mania ;

Feeling with the brain of my ape-like head ;

I'm getting back on the subway to-morrow...

---

[32] metro: subway train

[33] glean: to take small amounts

[34] satellite-framing (adverbs). [as opposed to verb-framing (ex. *enter*).]

Quotation 5

"Women are the gatekeepers of sexuality. But, men are the gatekeepers of relationship." —Susan Walsh

"O, while you live, tell truth and shame the devil!" —Shakespeare

"It is not the strongest of the species that survives, nor the most intelligent, but the one most responsive to change," —Darwin

"high-T"

Poem 5   *2011.*

The Iron Law of Morality

When what is right and what is true do not match, there cannot be a match.

No escap'n thru fleet'n feel'ns.
No pass'n of time can flee it.
No fun 'n lov'n can free it.
Truth's[35] mate is out there,
Is in there.
A'do'n th'dirty work.

'N one day,
As it always does,
Truth's mate came a'call'n.
A'pay'n cruel reality its due.
A'do'n th'dirty work.
Iron morality.

—Th'girl[36] sitt'n a'cry'n.
A'pay'n th'pain.
Nope—no escap'n.
Nature's cold iron judgement.
Th'girl sitt'n a'cry'n.
A'lone.

Ya see,
Th'man has gone a'way.
When he hearkened truth's mate a'call'n.
Th'man has gone a'way.
A'gain, as he always does.
...'N time's a'wast'n.

Ya see,
No loyalty here truth's mate told 'im.
B'cause what is past was what is pass'n.
What is actions tell th'next.
'N th'girl sitt'n a'cry'n.
A'lone.

'N th'man sitt'n a'sigh'n.
A'lone.
—A'heark'n....
B'cause, there's no escap'n,

---

[35] etymology: *trow*, *betroth*
[36] *The* cliticizes to the head noun.

When truth's mate comes a'call'n,
...A'one day.

Yeah, th'man has gone a'way.
When he heark'd truth's mate a'call'n.
Nope'a,
No escap'n,
Truth's mate's cruel algorithmic rul'n.
...'N time's a'waste'n.

Yeah, 'n th'girl sitt'n a'cry'n.
A'lone.
Th'man has gone a'way.
Nope escap'n, when he a'hearkend truth's mate a'call'n.
'N th'man sitt'n a'sigh'n.
A'lone.

Cold 'n cruel truth's mate,
Iron morality, came a'call'n.
A'do'n th'dirty-work.
'N th'girl sitt'n a'cry'n
A'lone.
Th'man has gone a'way.

Oh...
Th'poem,
        Th'poem,
                Th'poem.

There's[37] no escap'n it.

"...none but virgins marry..." —*Germania*, Tacitus, *150 BC*

---

[37] wikipedia.org/wiki/Elision

Quotation 6

"You must understand, the Jewish Communist leaders who took over Russia hated the Russian people. They hated Christians, and they tortured and slaughtered millions of Russians without a shred of human remorse. The October Revolution was not what you call in America the 'Russian Revolution'; it was indeed a Jewish invasion and a conquest over the Russian people." —Solzhenitsyn, *2002*

"as the spirit wanes, the form appears" —Bukowski, "Art*"*

A mutant hairless chimp.

Poem 6

Jus Primæ Noctis

Comrado. You banged a *virginalis* yester-day. *Sacer sanguis.*

Never surrender your morale. Hope in the invisible island, over the horizon. That way, that wise, someday you will reach the isle.

Now ; you will have yours. For-ever.

Freed from its abyss. —The sacred land. Attained.

Now fight the guilt.[38] Thou hast walked on *sacré* ground.

Stay or leave. Regardless. You know it's worth (*Marchette*[39]) and what it is.

A *terre* put there fore you by your fathers' choice though their Allfather's *Wille*, the *axis mundi*, [40] god inside the soul—*zum Grund des Seins*[41]—beyond the agendas and deceptions, thought[42] and taught—in turn put there by Selection.[43] Nature's will. —Truth independent, *algorithmic.* Fighting in the land of Man the chimpanzee.

"Virginity is the ideal of those who want to deflower." —Karl Kraus

---

[38] **shall (v.)** : O.E. *sceal* "I owe/he owes, will have to, ought to, must" (infinitive *sculan*, past tense *sceolde*), a common Germanic preterite-present verb, from P.Gmc. **skal-, *skul-* (cf. O.S.*sculan*, O.N., Swedish *skola*, M.Du. *sullen*, O.H.G. *solan*, Ger. *sollen*, Goth. *skulan* "to owe, be under obligation;" related via past tense form to O.E. *scyld* "guilt," Ger. *Schuld* "guilt, debt;").
Ground sense probably is "I owe," hence "I ought." The sense shifted in Middle English from a notion of "obligation" to include "futurity." Its past tense form has become ***should*** (*q.v.*). Cognates outside Germanic are Lith. *skeleti* "to be guilty," *skilti* "to get into debt;" Old Prussian *skallisnan* "duty," *skellants* "guilty."
[39] https://en.wikipedia.org/wiki/Merchet
[40] *axis mundi*: turning point of the world in Hindu religion —line through the world's centre around which the universe revolves —*the soul.*
[41] "Ground of being" is a reference to Paul Tillich.
[42] *Denken*
[43] A reference to Darwin's Selection in evolution.

Quotation 7

"Verily, I swear, 'tis better to be lowly born, and range with humble livers in content, than to be perk'd up in a glistering grief, and wear a golden sorrow." —Shakespeare, *Henry VIII*

"It is no measure of health to be well adjusted to a profoundly sick society." —Krishnamurti

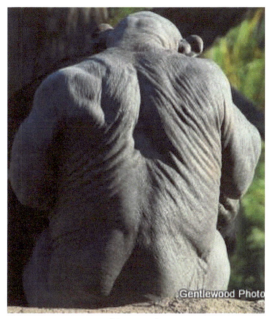

Mesomorph

Poem 7 *2011.*
For Getting

> An event changes the meaning of things. —Heidegger

> "a truth emerges only through the appearing of an event" —Alain Badiou

> "In the beginning was not the Word, but the Deed." —Goethe's Faust says at adventure start

If he could put a word upon the track.
If he could use an operator[44] to put down a logic set upon a fact.
Then the logic, the if-then chain, would be getting his way.
Then the position—the proposition[45]—would be understood.
So overcome. (Regardless, for logically truly or falsely does not mean rightly or wrongly.[46])
He looked and he dug. Puzzling over and under. The patterns or no patterns.
The thoughts and the their words. The command, logic.
He wondered and groped in the park. And groped not and walked and wandered.
In stupor.
Time not like an exist. Exist not as a time.
Tumbling towards an emotion. Out on a motion, at least.
And so, in this moment,
The action. Something out of nothing.
—The monkey grasped the ripe banana.
Like a noun begets a verb and a verb begets a binary.[47]
Between the tumbling to forgotten.

---

[44] A logical operator.
[45] Referring to the (often exploited) propositional fallacy of logic.
[46] Referring to the propositional fallacy of logic.
[47] noun ('nom') is Latin for *name.* …All predicates create binaries, not nouns.

Quotation 8

"When one lives with wolves, one must learn how to howl." —Russ proverb

Very few people would ever fall in love if they never read about it. —para. Foucault

White skinned hairless chimp

Poem 8   *2011/12/12.*

The Dover Wolf [48]

A Criticism of Life :   *For the Jew Anthony Hecht,* "The Dover Bitch"

       "Homo homini lupus est." (Man is wolf to man.)

So there sat this ageing "friend," let's call him Matthew Arnold, and me in a seaboard *café*
With the white cliffs of Greenwich Mean Time crumbling away behind us,
And I said to him,

"Girls are players ;   stealing your time.
Stealers is what most girls are—because they are 'only human.'
Stealing your time.   Stealing your time away—your life away.   Spending your
time—spending your life.
And taking your time is taking your money even if you never spend 'a penny' (on 'em).
Stealing your information, intelligence, data, opinions, network.
Stealing your entertainment ;   getting an adventure ;   an education.
'Getting one over on you'—'getting off on you.'   Stealing it all.
'Ripping off' your life[49] and your pride.
Not paying for it—not giving their sexual favours.
Stealers.   Stealing your time.
See them for what they are up to :   *Stealing your time.*
Only then can you defend yourself—
From being their victim of their thieving.   Stealing your time, spending your time.
...Your want makes you the target.   And they target the weak ;
Because only the wanting, the lacking, can be had—
       Used,
            Exploited.
               'A piece of meat.'
'Only human'—amoral as a wolf, *'Why not,'* she predicates the prey to herself and does not
question. (When she answered with the Rhetorical Question to herself, 'Why not' :   Like
Nietzsche warned, 'If you have a *why*, you can bear any *how*.' —Every 'why not' has a how.
And every *how* has a 'for *who* (profits)?'. Because 'who, what, when, where, why, and
[w]how' are all just different cases, different case forms of the same functional-pronoun
word.)
Fool, they will drain all the blood from your body, if you let them ;
And then they will suck (out) the marrow from your bones, if you let them.
—While they look at you with litigiously innocent eyes and 'play nice.'
So you must not be *passiva*.   Defend yourself by playing a tight game.   —Controlling every
minute and every bloody drop of info.
Both sides always timing to be able to defend a 'game theoretic' defection.[50]

---

[48] "The Dover Bitch" by the Jew Anthony Hecht, was a parody of "The Dover Beach" by Arnold.
[49] opportunity cost
[50] Game Theory: branch of maths applied to evolution, behaviour & politics. The analysis of a situation involving conflicting interests (as in business or military strategy) in terms of gains & losses among opposing players.

Her stealthy scamming—hiding her agenda with flirts and niceties ;
After all, she has a man and, for what she owes you,
Will never ever
Pay you
      With her sexual favours
         For stealing
            Your time.
Be disillusioned![51] On-guard! Let those wolfish thieves—those stealthy cheaters—steal
nothing! Naught a thing!
...Before you even decide to enter the *café* to coffee with them, *suss them out*,
About boyfriend, why meet, what want.
—If a user, on-the-take, then only say, 'Yes, I understand. I don't have time. *I don't have time.*'
Outed, caught, they know *time*. They know and they make a quick retreat.
And you saved your time.
You see, you got it all wrong : girls ain't 'bitches' ; they're wolves.
Young fertile white-women are treated like gods. —Women are looked at as gods. —Men
are invisible. Gynocentric men orbit women like male dancing pigeons and talk and perform
and slave away. While the woman pigeon just quietly stands there. *Man* 'is the nigger of the
world.'"

Anyway, I said all this to my buddy in that seaboard *café*,
Running to fat, and we commiserated and agreed and strategised and shared info.
"And wouldn't you know," "you should know," months later,
When he was back in his hometown and didn't have any game theoretic need of using me
anymore,
I emailed him to do me a small but slightly inconvenient favour—no reply.[52]

    Roughly Peatro's statistical eighty percent[53] of the times you were ripped off and you
    were scammed and you never ever even knew it. —Definition of stealing.

a dancing pigeon

—Evidencing that much of what is going on is largely focused on the issue of "defection" & defection prevention.
[51] To no longer have illusions.
[52] The last period of a game is a one-shot game where the dominant strategy is to defect ("cheating"). Therefore it
helps (cooperation) to have a future.
[53] Pareto Principle 80/20 or 50/01, the square root law

Quotation 9

"'They are born, then put in a box; they go home to live in a box; they study by ticking boxes; they go to what is called 'work' in a box, where they sit in their cubicle box; they drive to the grocery store in a box to buy food in a box; they go to the gym in a box to sit in a box; they talk about thinking 'outside the box'; and when they die they are put in a box,' he writes. 'All boxes, Euclidean, geometrically smooth boxes.'" —Taleb

"For the Jews, the God of the Old Testament is nothing more or less than the racially pure Jewish gene pool." —Kevin B. MacDonald

Hunter gatherer

Poem 9   *2011/12/22. metro Kreshatik.*

The No-Poem People

This big, liquid drop of poem I saw outside to-day.

The no-poem[54] people.

Everywhere, the no-poem people ; the "... drone-like individuals…" (Nietzsche)

Following the straw-man[55] politic media that no-poem people would follow.

Watching the movies that no-poem people would like to watch.

Talking the talk that no-poem people would talk.

Not talking—the way a no-poem person would not talk.

Harkening to the songs that no-poem people would harken to.

Reading the stories that no-poem people would read.

Acting the way that no-poem people would act.

Doing the things that no-poem people would do.

Thinking the way that no-poem people would think.

Not helping, the way a no-poem individual would not help—not responsibly (answering), not bravely or not unpopular ; but helping for a popular, obsequious cause in the way a no-poem individual would.

Believing the way that no-poem people would believe.

Leading the lives that no-poem people would follow.

Mother, father, relations, mates, strangers, crowds... People, person, you.

On the streets or in the markets. See them all!

They are all the no-poem people.

> "We think all other people zeros,
> And integers : ourselves alone." —Pushkin, *Onegin*

> "They reach me not, touch me some edge or that,
> But reach me not and all my life's become
> One flame, that reaches not beyond
> My heart's own hearth,
> Or hides among the ashes there for thee.
> 'Thee'? Oh, 'Thee' is who cometh first
> Out of mine own soul-kin,
> For I am homesick after mine own kind
> And ordinary people touch me not.
> And I am homesick
> After mine own kind that know, and feel
> And have some breath for beauty and the arts." —Ezra Pound, "In Durance", *Personae* (*1909*)

---

[54] "Poem" comes from the Greek word for poem —which is rooted in the Greek root word for create.

[55] straw dog: Something that is made only to be destroyed. (Origin: **Straw dogs** were used as ceremonial objects in ancient China. Chapter 5 of the *Tao Te Ching* begins with the lines "Heaven & Earth are heartless / treating creatures like straw dogs". Su Ch'e comments "Heaven & Earth are not partial. They do not kill living things out of cruelty or give them birth out of kindness. We do the same when we make straw dogs to use in sacrifices. We dress them up & put them on the altar, but not because we love them. & when the ceremony is over, we throw them into the street, but not because we hate them.")

Quotation 10

" *'America is a propositional nation with a 'living constitution'* — A 'propositional nation' is a dictatorship. Whoever controls the 'proposition' and can change the 'living constitution' is the dictator." —Weisse

"*Shalom* does not mean peace, reconciliation or harmony. It's accurate English translation is 'security for the Jews.'" —the Jew Gilad Atzmon

"Muriel Rukeyser wrote "[Ballad of Orange and Grape](#)"[...]. The poem reflects one of the central concerns of her life and art—the power of language to shape the world's realities."

Poison gas and concentration camps is just so much more spooky and dramatic and exceedingly woeful and guilty than bombs — dropped from a long distance on civilians in Gaza and in Dresden and in Hiroshima. —E. E. E.

"...hominids—clamouring for citizenship." —James Boyle, *Shamans, Software and Spleens*

Poem 10 *2011.*

Propositional[56] [57] Chosenness[58]

wars that were wars that are wars to be

the conquered in mind pay the tribute[59] to the tribe of the conquer

slaves[60] minding in mind and will to the masters in mind and might

and the slave resents the insult

controlled and forced and coerced as he is

anti[61] is blamed whom's[62] emotion[63]

the annual[64] tribute of billions to the self-chosen[65] master

are the riches of health-cares and pensions not afforded in the tribute yielders' usaland[66]

words that were words that are words to be

. . . . .

In re, regarding the wars. Or regarding history as it is framed[67] and *worded*
To you.
—Regarding the reification[68] issue of : "Is history a lie?" Or politics. Or correctness norms.
Just ask yourself this about your personal life you've lived and learned :
"Do men lie and betray?"   ...So reframe, re-think, re-word, revisionist.

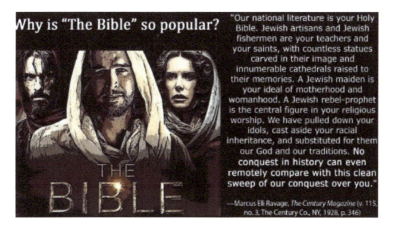

---

[56] A reference to a fallacy of logic referred to in Logic as the "propositional fallacy (affirming the consequent)".
[57] propositions: wikipedia.org/wiki/Vacuous_truth
[58] Godel's Incompleteness Theorems: Any system as powerful as ...[a] theory which can prove its own consistency is necessarily inconsistent. (a.k.a.: self-reference.)
[59] The Greek practice & etymology of *tribute* is tribe.
[60] Hegel's Master-slave dialectic
[61] word origin of *anti*: "in front of and facing".
[62] "Who — whom." (or "Who does what to whom?") ~ The central question of politics, according to Lenin.
[63] Ancient Polish proverb: "The Jew strikes you and cries out in pain."
[64] A reference to the 8 billion dollars submitted annually (9 million dollars per day) by the citizens of the USA to the Jewish-only citizens of the ethno state of Israel for the past 80 years; & for the never ending future years. (& multi-trillions of dollars annually on wars & subsidies by USA on Muslim nations for "The Jewish State" security.)
[65] A reference to *LOVE THY NEIGHBOR: The evolution of in-group morality* — a scientific deconstruction of "The Chosen (favourite) Race of God" as self-proposed by the tribal Judean scribes in Babylonia who authored the politico-legend Laws of racial supremacy and separatism—the Torah (Law) (—like the *Laws of Manu.*).
[66] The way Africans call U.S.A. and Americans: "ooosaa-land" and "ooosaa-man"
[67] wikipedia.org/wiki/Framing_(social_sciences)
[68] Reification is the act of treating something abstract as if it were a concrete, physical entity. It's a fallacy of ambiguity that can occur when someone ascribes a definitive form or value to an abstract concept.

Quotation 11

"Nothing in its place is bad; nothing out of its place is good," —Whitman

"Throughout history the poets and philosophers, the leaders of industry and science, the leading lights of art and culture, statesmen and economists whose blood was not infected by the Jews have warned against the Jew in every century. They proclaimed openly and clearly what he is: the plague. From Tacitus to Schopenhauer, from Giordano Bruno to Mommsen and Treitschke, the intellectual heroes of every age have called the Jew the demon of decay, the ferment of decomposition, as the misfortune of the peoples or of humanity. In the New Testament, the Jews were in Christ's words the 'sons of the Devil.'" (Esser, *Ibid*, pg. 10)

Back-rest

Poem 11 *2008.*

In and Out[69] [70]

Every thing is in and out ;
And with in there is no other.[71]

In is in and in is inned ;
Be cause out is out and out is outed, my friend.

And in is on and win is won ;
Just like out is off[72] and oust[73] is lost,[74] my friend.

All of the outs in there ;
If'n[75] you "get it."

Then, as you ought,[76] no[77] doubt[78] you'll see ;
The ins and outs to be or not[79] to be.[80]

> "The whole world is like one big intercourse—everything is in and
> out—smoking, eating, stabbing." —Susan Atkins glossing Manson

---

[69] This poem is about my *independent* etymological observation as a youth that a huge amount of words (especially prefixes of words) in English have origines in words that meant the position "in" or the position "out" (or *on* or *off*). Thus most of the words in this poem have words or parts of words that can be traced back to ancient forms of the words that meant in or out.
…[wikipedia.org/wiki/Deconstruction : "…Derrida then sees this differences, as elemental oppositions (0-1), working in all 'languages', all 'systems of distinct signs', all 'codes', where terms don't have an 'absolute' meaning, but can only get it from reciprocal determination with the other terms (1-0). This structural difference is the first component that Derrida will take into account when articulating the meaning of *différance*, a mark he felt the need to create & will become a fundamental tool in his lifelong work: deconstruction."]
[70] " the algebra of logic *par excellence*, or the Boolean algebra. This algorithm, like the binary arithmetic, is based on the dichotomy, the choice between *yes* and *no*, the choice between being in a class and outside." —Wiener
[71] Likely derived from the root word for "out".
[72] Likely derived from the root word for "out".
[73] Likely derived from the root word for "out".
[74] Likely derived from the root word for "out".
[75] Likely derived from the root word for "out".
[76] Likely derived from the root word for "out".
[77] Likely derived from the root word for "out". — & double negatives negate a negative —in tongues . In multiplicative maths, two negative numbers make a positive number.
[78] Likely derived from the root word for "out".
[79] Etymology of *not* is "no-wit". & "no" has *some* etymological relation to the root word for out or off.
[80] "When He Came In"

Quotation 12

"For whoever has, to him more shall be given; and whoever does not have, even what he has shall be taken away from him." —*Mark 4;25*

"The child that you choose to have is the message that you send to the future." —unknown

"Indra stands accused." —Sir Mortimer Wheeler

Chimps do not do this. Only Bonobo Chimps do this.

Poem 12 *2012/2/11.*
Hitting the Words
Hitting the words
Right through
To
The real.
Real right words
Hitting right through
To the real you.
From the real me.
For a moment or a mood or two.
It can be
Clear, right through.
From me to you.

...One rare word, one rare line
Gets it right ;
Hits it through
From he, the writer, to you.
But it takes two.

...That day I spoke real and right to you,
My words could not hit at who was not there.
And that word I hit that was right,
When you read, found there to be nothing to you.

> "Those who hear and do not understand are like the deaf. Of them the
> proverb says: 'Present, they are absent.'" —Heraclitus

Quotation 13

"...every word being an idea..." —Rimbaud

"Never do business with a religious son-of-a-bitch. His word ain't worth a shit—not with the Good Lord telling him how to fuck you on the deal." —W. Burroughs

"You can't tell anybody anything that they don't know already." —William Burroughs

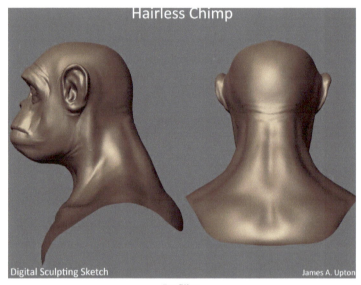

Profiling

Poem 13 *2012/2/13. metro Chernihivska.*

I'm Still Alive

! —I'm still alive.

My mind beats, "I'm still alive."

Wow, still, through it all.

I walk the street again.

Bright, bright, morning sun, shining.

I see the show again.

I'm in the movie again.

My identification—in it again.

I'm living in it again.

Alive!

Before it's over, (dead),

I'm in it again.

I woke up this morning again, sun shining brightly, I walk the street again, seeing.

Still alive.[81]

All over again.

Once more.

Fathers before,

       Sons after,

           Me now.

My ID—in this thing again, is seeing ;

Flicker of this moment ; now ;

---

[81] "the quick"

Quotation 14

"Whose secret Presence, through Creation's veins
Running Quicksilver-like eludes your pains;
Taking all shapes from Mah to Mahi; and
They change and perish all—but He remains;" —Omar Khayyam

"The grandest forms of active force
From Tao come, their only source." —Lao-tzu

Hominid

Poem 14 *2012/4/2.*
Under Love

> "There's always one who loves and one who lets himself be loved." —Maugham, *Of Human Bondage.* There are two types of people. One type of character is searching for someone to love. The other type of character is searching for someone to love him.

I reject you, I reject you, I reject you. And you love[82] me, love me, love me.

I give you nothing. And you offer your body and *femme*.

I tell you to leave. And you are there.

I send you no hello's, far be it. And you send me I love you's, often.

I bought you nothing and took you nowhere. And you arrived at my door.

I say good-bye. And you say hello.

I'm not there. And you won't stop.

I terminate you, I disappear, months or year. And I can't escape you.

I neglect you, I neglect you, I neglect you. And you darling me, darling me, darling me.

Because one thing, one little thing, is, sadly, true.

I'll be the only honourable mate you'll have ever known.

---

[82] love: the mating drive

Quotation 15

"A time is coming when men will go mad, and when they see someone who is not mad, they will attack him, saying, 'You are mad; you are not like us.'" —St. Antony the Great

"Fertilisation is all about genetics. Development is all about epigenetics." —Sapolsky

"I'm *the man*."

Poem 15 *2012/11/5.*
Mode to Dada

> "Dada aimed to destroy the reasonable deceptions of man and
> recover the natural and unreasonable order." —Hans Arp

hi, tiptop b-beat in the da da du mm mmm of ahhh.

sounds referring to sights.

tag a word a reference to things, acts.

o growl hoot bla tip top tap[83] dot. ug!

i say see this, that. —You think this that, do.

laughing, howl, hum, apa[84] snarl hiss click mu.[85]

see, smell, emote, move, twitch frown down blink.

tag, tag.

a touch, attach word thought on you, is attack.[86]

ha-ha, hoo-hoo, word, tag, soothe trust smile.

unt-uh but.

a-ha give.

me, tell spell take.

you, taught think believe lose.

now leaving, utter[87] sound, bye-bye.

---

[83] An *ablaut*.

[84] "*Ape*, from Old English *apa*, is an onomatopoetic imitation of animal chatter."

[85] "...*mu* is an ancient Zen answer which, when given to a question, un-asks the question." "...rejects premises of the question, which are that one or the other must be chosen." —*The Mind's I*

[86] *Tact, tactic, attack, attach, take, touche* —all derive from the word for touch.

[87] *Utter* means to speak; & is etymologically traced back to the word *out*.

Quotation 16

"…the passion of laughter is nothing else but a sudden glory arising from sudden conception of some eminency in ourselves, by comparison with the infirmities of others, or with our own formerly…" —Hobbes

"Let us part happily, fate wins." —*Edda*

Man was created in God's image. —Genesis, *Torah* (Law)

Poem 16 *2012/6.*
Things Change

       "A rat done bit my sister [...] and Whitey's on the moon." (youtube.com/watch?v=goh2x_G0ct4)

Son, I am from back in the days when girls did not cut their pubic-hair.

Not one girl. Never had the thought.

Now even the men cut their pubic-hair.

Back when I was young, even the women in porno had full pubic-hair.

And we barely saw any porno, back then, before the internet.

And in the *1980*'s not one man or woman, of any age, had a single tattoo ; then "the dam broke." And, until *2001*, no man had a beard or mustache ; not a one. (And no tattoos.)

Things change, things were not always like this—may-be you didn't know that things

    Were not always

        This way.

The world changed overnight from the internet porno.

I am from, back, before, the internet.

Back when I was young, Europeans were the majority in America,

And in Europe.

Things were not always like this.

Hell, 50% of girls were maidenheads by 21 (women would get husbands),

Back when I was young.

We had no mobile phones!

Internet and mobile phones and racial dispossession.

As political landscapes dissolve[88]

Men as meme mimicking machines.

Things change. A lot. (Things change—not by chance, not by accident, not naturally, but by elites' chosen policies.)

It was not like, this, back in my generation.

Hell, there were less than 4 billion people on earth when I was born.

Now it's twice that—while hypocritical "green" environmentalism has skyrocketed ("open-borders" population explosion coming from "the global South").

And I am only 40 years eld ;

Born in *1970*—that was before the Holocaust.[89] And after the *Holodomor*[90] that will never be.

Back when I was a young child, in America, there were *negros*, almost every one was. (Miscegenation was against the law.) Now there are no *negros*—only *mulattos*.

Everyone on TV was *blanco*—America was 90% *blanco*—England 99%—try to think that reality frame—but I know that you cannot. ...With "the whiteman" walking on the moon.

Things change.

Things war.

Things win,

Things lose.

---

[88] A sampling from the *dinosauria, we* poem by Bukowski.
[89] books.google.com/ngrams/graph?content=Holocaust&year_start=1945&year_end=2023
[90] HOLOCAUST and HOLODOMOR, Nicholas Lysson

...Things—*thoughts*.

The way things are to-day—things were not always this way.

Things change. Things don't stay the same.

Son, may-be you never realised that. May-be you didn't know.

I was around back then ; I know.

Back when I was born, White America had the highest average personal income in the world (and was the largest *creditor* country in the world),[91] and could put men on the moon…

"In those years, [...] where we stood, saying I."[92]

I see them on the road, and I try to tell them, "what's what." *Me* and my "imaginary friends".

"The Thinker"

[91] gnosticliberationfront.com/America_The_Grim_Truth.htm

[92] A sampling from the poem, *In Those Years*.

Quotation 17

"Iron by iron is sharpened. And a man sharpens the face of his friend." —*Proverbs* & *Hávamál*

"The secret to happiness in life is to find a woman with low expectations." —Buffet
"In my whole life, I have known no wise people (over a broad subject matter area) who didn't read all the time. None, zero." —Munger

"...anti-paranoia, when nothing is connected to anything,..." —*Gravity's Rainbow*

"The sacred bond."

Poem 17 *2012/6.*

Off of Me

What is in my mind that I don't know about that is going to come together into a poem?

What monologue have I been thinking over and over, but I don't notice it?

Or what spark of anger will posit on a puzzle-piece to posit out?

Birth-pangs from nowhere ; not there, but there.

Off of me,

   You poem!

I wrote you,

   Now you are off of me.

Domain taken ; owned ; deeded, archived, permanent ; legacy.

Off of me, equals freedom ; a weight off.

A primatising freedom.

Poetry—a way to utter[93] it off.

Off of me, you poem!

I bore you, now you are out of me.

When did this hole open up? When will it stop?

There is no final poem.[94]

> *"and it will keep on doing it*
> *until you die or it dies in you."* [95]

---

[93] out

[94] As Chomsky says, language (information, cognition) is recursive.

[95] From *so you want to be a writer*, Bukowski.

Quotation 18

"What's it all about? You know what I mean?" —*Alfie* (1966)

"Frost, snow, rain, sun. From all the seasons I have something to learn." Said the eunuch to the judges of the Chinese emperor when they would go question the eunuch in prison about what he thought about the emperor locking him up in prison.

"The normal fuck by a normal man is taken to be an act of invasion and ownership undertaken in a mode of predation…" —Andrea Dworkin, *Intercourse*

Man's best friend

Poem 18 *2012/6.*

Strays

A poem can be transparent—with no simile, no symbolism, no syllogism.

It is a real fact,

That the cities in Russian-speaking Europe, have stray dogs around,

Sleeping around outside, with no masters.

We all[96] there watch them and see them.

The stray dogs trailing after the bitches,

Running after the bitches,

Sniffing the butts of the bitches,

Licking the butts of the bitches,

Chasing the bitches,

Jumping on the bitches

—On the street.

Diseased in body the bitches. (From bacterium to virus.)

No master and no pack.

Making more mutts the bitches. Like themselves.

Masterless, packless, breedless, and worthless.

Disgraced and dirty.

I'm not talking about people—I'm talking about real dogs.

That is the real way it is there ;

Dogs let loose ;

Dogs gone astray.

And nobody cares.

---

[96] logical quantifier: (logic) a word (such as 'some' or 'all' or 'no' or 'exactly' or 'at least' or 'at most') that binds the variables in a logical proposition.

Quotation 19

Objective facts are game theoretic Shelling points in the contest of competing wills. —E.E.E.

I act on facts not plans.[97] —E.E.E.

Everything is primatology. —E.E.E.

All thoughts are chess. —E.E.E., YouTube.com/watch?v=5dKCK8SRUKU

Humans are the example of the universe's recursion: a bundle of atoms complexly arranged to *consciously* look at the universe of atoms, itself. —E.E.E. YouTube.com/watch?v=r5aaBDbHl8I

Sex without commitment is the masculine analog to sex without love. ...This covers 99% of all sexual encounters with a new partner. —E.E.E.

Most abortions are the result of hypergamy. To hinder access to abortion is to dampen women's access to hypergamy. —E.E.E.

Not a chimp. Not a human. A gorilla.

---

[97] "IBM scientists found a way to power chips with ionic currents, streams of charged molecules that operate in an 'event driven' way like the human brain."

Poem 19 *2012/6.*

To All the Women Who Will Never Have Husbands

I often wonder about you, them, the 80 percent. —All you

Young-women (old "women over 35 are invisible") who will never attain a permanent husband. I often

Think about you women. And I know you women have

No idea.

All you women don't know.

You women don't know it, but, you will far be it have life husbands.

And you won't have families, if families mean fathers in the home. But

You will have one bastard child or two.

Your daughters also won't have husbands.[98]

And the daughters won't have families, if families mean "fathers in the home". But

Your daughters will have one bastardised child or two.

Yes, it is the moral breakdown of a folk, and decline.

Biologically, men cannot husband women's promiscuity. —Women who aimed too high for their mate.[99] So they remain men and not husbands. Tackling woman after woman.

Girlfriend after girlfriend. Relationship after relationship. —Fuck-buddy after f-buddy. Not building.[100]

Men with no families are not optimal workers.[101]

And women's bastardised children without fathers are poorly invested in and poorly regulated. And it all goes on into decline.

All you women, don't you know the big secret?

Eighty percent of all you women will far be it have a long-term husband. That's the justice.

And it was woman's choice and women actively chose it. Because women are the gatekeepers of sexuality. And, secretly, men are the gatekeepers of relationship. That's the justice. And that is the big secret going on.

Too late now, but women would have been happier to marry young and have love long-term, by aiming lower combined with chastity. Embarrassing to say it.

...But 10 percent do aim low enough. And the other 10 percent were the top 10 percent.

---

[98] etymology: house-bond to a *hausfau*
[99] hypergamy. Duras, *The Lover*)
[100] wikipedia.org/wiki/R/K_selection_theory
[101] J. D. Unwin

Quotation 20

"Power is not a means, it is an end." —Orwell., *1984*
"And yet it is also true that one can write nothing readable unless one constantly struggles to efface one's own personality. Good prose is like a windowpane." —*ibid.*

"A 'slum' is not a place, it is people." —jewamongyou.com

"History is past politics, and politics is present history." —EA Freeman

"Words are men's daughters, but God's sons are things." —S. Madden

Breaking the law

Poem 20 *2012/7. Lviv.*

Haunted Lviv

Walking the streets all day.

In the center. The centre.

Looking at the old and dilapidated buildings in the centre.

Falling apart. Crumbling, olden, haunting.

Holding ghosts forgotten, stories forgotten ;

Possessing folks erased, histories erased.

The stone streets. Who made them? What menfolk? When, what year?

No one tells and no one knows.

The old buildings. Who made them and when?

No one knows, no one wants to know. They[102] want to not know.

There is an active disinterest that is telling.

Every day, walking and looking, I think of the ghosts. The folks who once sat in these shops. And central parks and buildings.

The evil ghosts of history. History is a lie, the victors ; convention and politics, what folks think they think—it's all a lie.

Every ancient building in the centre is telling out a story.[103] To no one. And every old cobble stone street.

Who laid these stones? What's the story?

The story is dead. And no one knows it. Active ignorance ; purposeful.

The population of Lviv city is entirely Ukraïna now.

But just fifty and one hundred years ago, Lvov was called Lemberg and part of Galacia Österreich.

Every man on the street was Deutschen or Polen. And spoke Deutsch. Imagine. ...Sipping in "the Viennese coffee house."

Every building shop (*магазин*, *sklep*, *Geschäft*) and stone road in the center was built by Deutsche. (From today's Town Hall and street plan to today's train station. —Annexed by Austria.)

They brought the "Magdeburg *Recht*"[104] city *platz* design and *strasse*, buildings, chocolatier, Viennese coffee houses, *Bierbrauerei*, Opera *haus*...

Now, not one man in the city has a Deutsche or Polak surname, patrimony.

The Österreichisches Deutsche were all ethnically cleansed, when Deutschland, Österreich, and Ukraïna lost WWI. (But almost all of Deutsche had already left after the "1867 Compromise".)

Then the city became only *Polacy*.

Then Deutschland lost WWII, and every *Polak* and *Polka* was ethnically cleansed from the city (by Moscow edict). And replaced with Ukraïner, only.

Somewhere, far away, in the Deutschen and *Polakem* graves are buried the keys to all the centre shops and buildings of Lwów.

---

[102] *They* is a bound variable. —*They* is sometimes used singularly and sometimes plurally (and genderless).

[103] "The city was arranged according to the Magdeburg Laws" —lvivcenter.org/en/lia/objects/latin-cathedral/

[104] https://magdeburg-law.com

But all the folks in Lviv are Ukraïner now, and half-Ruski Ukraïner. Sipping in "*das Wiener Kaffeehaus.*" And *Bier* brewery shops and liquid chocolatier cafes in the *ancien régime* (*Szlachta*) buildings lining the stone streeted "*Rynok*" square (*platz*).

Aliens. Populating alias buildings they did not build.

Occupying stolen land. An other stolen Jerusalem—Palestinians framed as philistine and removed ; dispossessed ; *le Grand Replacement.*

"What are you doing here? Why are you here? ...Do you like my country?", the Ukraïner *colonos* say to all the exilic *Europer* tourists.

Only half-Ruski Ukraïner now—and the buildings crumbling. Crumbling down.

And the Ukraïner swear and believe and teach that Lviv is the cradle of, and centre of, and origin of, their *Kultur.*

But the old buildings and stone streets remain.

Cover-up, history, but these gravestones to extinct folks stand.

The old buildings and stone streets in the centre of Lemberg,[105]

Are ghostly,

   Wondering,

     Possessed.

Crumbling *dinosauria* fossils.

There it stands, looking like a "little *Wien.*"[106] (But the Ukrainians/Ruthians, speaking Slavonic mixed with Polski then Ruski, all call it, a "little Paris.")

At the centre, I "walk the rounds," reading the buildings ;

Buildings telling stories

And nobody harkens and nobody reads and nobody knows.

> "The name is ul. Konarskiego now,
> although the unkempt building still speaks German." —Leo Yankevich

---

[105] The city had the name, Lemberg (Lion-city). When the ethnic Deutsche who built the city were eradicated from the city, the name was changed to the Slavic name, Lviv and Lvov and Lwow (Lion-city).

[106] Ukrainians dub Lviv "the Little Paris". But it does not look like a little Paris. It looks exactly like a little Vienna.

Quotation 21

"What is a traitor? ...Why, one that swears and lies." —*Macbeth*

When a man says he ranks a woman as a 10, what it really means is that he would rank the satisfaction of his ego as a 10 if he was looking in her face as he had an orgasm in her vagina. Which translates into, she is how he wants his issue (offspring) to look (as Kant or H.C. Anderson said). —E. E. E.

Body language

Poem 21   *2012/7/17.*
See Through the See-through
Chimps look at humans and only see humans ;
But once in a while they see the chimp in his face.

Humans look at chimps and only see chimps ;
But once in a while they see the human in his face.

And, once in the wile,
Humans look at humans and they see through
And see the chimp in the face of humans.
Seeing through and seeing the see-through.

Humans look at the news media and the entertainment and the advertising and politics and
discursive and only see that.
But some see through it and see the agenda and the deception and identity-politics and
primatology in the face of it all.
Seeing through and seeing the see-through.

Poem 22   *2012/7/26. metro Mydan*
The Going On *Cantos*
        "You must go on. I can't go on. I'll go on." —Samuel Beckett, *The Unnamable*

Ezra Pound's *cantos* chants, "Master thyself, then others shall thee beare."

God your life your soul
this spirit that you flesh
weakened and cowered though it be.
How to be with all the disasters?
The humiliations and your stupidities?
How to erase the minding mind?
There is a sorrow
as you sit on the street-bench and look out.
This life you've lived, what a joke, almost 40 years of pitiless cumber.
Stunned, you sit and watch the people, buildings.
People—what wretches.
Chimpanzees[107] are not humans—humans are chimpanzees.
From in these lowest bottoms
you remember.
You remember other bottoms
moods and outs that turned upward, somehow.
Damages can be gotten over
though it seems and feels not,
everything can change, does.

---

[107] troglodytes

Hold on,
steady, cool.
There will be a turn, up.
Out there another opening opportunity to mount
and damages can be gotten over.
Keep going on.
Scarred, damaged, and lost lots
toughened and wizened and wary,
just keep going on,
going on with your life,
unto[108] "the bitter end."

I see you, through the smoke pouring from cars, you're walking. I beare you.

> "If you can force your heart and nerve and sinew
> To serve your turn long after they are gone,
> And so hold on when there is nothing in you
> Except the will which says to them: 'Hold on!'" (Kipling)

· · · · ·

You're one-hundred dead men lying on the dirt.
You're everyman dead lying on the dirt.
Dead so many times you can sit in a chair and turn around and look back at yourself, without moving. Back at that pretty young-man, dead.
Dead so many times. Killed mostly ; by thieving lies ; and neglect.

---

[108] Etymologically, unto means onto.

Quotation 22

"Little women are for loving. Big women are for working." —Ruski proverb

"Even snakes lie together." —D.H. Lawrence

In physics, *Quanta* ("quantum leaps": electrons are here or there and nowhere in-between—a particularism analogous to Aristotle's law of the excluded middle) exist but *Qualia* do not exist. So physics's *Quanta* are analogous to a philosophy of mind using a particularism interpretation and physics's *Qualia* are analogous to a philosophy of mind using a universalism interpretation. ...The analogy works well because *quanta* are the ultimate **particulars** of the physical world. *Qualia*, conversely, can be seen as representing the **universal** nature of subjective experience: For example, the redness of a rose's colour and the redness of a stop sign are instances of the same universal quality—the *quale* of "redness." ...**The Problem of the Universal:** Philosophers (like C. I. Lewis, who popularised the term) have noted that *qualia* are "a sort of **universals**" because a single quality can be repeated in different individual experiences; meaning they are characteristics that are the *same* across different instances. ...This frames the **mind-body problem** as a contest between an **atomistic, particularistic approach** (physics/*quanta*) and a **holistic, universalistic approach** (phenomenology/*qualia*). —E. E. E. from AI

Lothario

Poem 23 *2012/7/30.*
Writing the Story

And he was born American.

And he could have lived out that story. But he didn't.

He left. He got out.

He "turned over a new leaf."

He didn't want to die that way.

He wasn't going to go out[109] that way.

He wasn't going to go to and fro ;

To work from home… Round and round, until it was over.

Until he died of old age.

For nothing ; piling money.

"I'm not going out this way," he uttered from his bed one day.

And, by dint[110] of anger's courage, he rose up and faced down the fear—and he stopped.

He got up out from underneath his story.[111]

Bad story.

Becoming the author,

Not a character following a plot to a destination, a destiny.

He started a new story. A better story.

Went to new destinations ; adventures. "Sailing to Byzantium."[112]

Growing. Writing a new story.

An interesting story. A creative story. A better story.

Than the one he was in.

Poem 24 *2012/8/11.*
The Justice in the World

And you wonder if life is fair? And why life is not fair?

And you wonder a feel that there is no justice in the universe?

I am the only justice in the universe. *You* are the only justice in the universe. *And injustice.*

Every time you don't give a real relationship to a promiscuous girl, there is justice in the universe. Nature's.

Your morality and action is the judge and dispenser of justice. Your morality is the only morality that exists in the universe.

You are it. Nothing outside it.

You are the lawman and marshal.

Every time you nix someone who disrespects you, cheats you. There is justice done in the universe, more.

And every time you do not, there is no justice in the universe, less ; and life is unfair.

Algorithms of millions of years of Life's truth and workings

     Cognate as justice through my thoughts and emotions and doings.

---

[109] "Go out" is an English expression that means "to die".

[110] Force or effort; power.

[111] wikipedia.org/wiki/Negative_Capability

[112] "*[West] …no country for old men. …[East]*"

And when you do what is right—for you, in your world—against the world's lies—Nature's hammer falls—there can even be that ecstatic moment. When god is alive, incarnate. And justice reigns supreme.

> "It's tragic how few people ever possess their souls before they die. Nothing is more rare in any man, than an act of his own. It is quite true. Most people are other people." —Oscar Wilde

Poem 25 *2012/9/9.*

A Little Tingle and a Squirt

A little tingle and a squirt and it's over.

My desire for you. And I feel empty

From the nothing

That is you, us. Now feeling the sad, again.

Wishing nothing was something,

Our relation

—Our compatibility. And I scurry how to posit

A thought to

Escape you ;

Free of this bed, us. I think how it is,

It is that we have nothing in common. And I anger at,

If you want a relationship,

"Why don't you choose someone you have something in-common with?"

Or develop yourself up for it. (Try to pursue one of my hobbies.)

Why!

Not nothing. And I bolt,

Away. Seeking after something, more. Again.

...And her female-hypergamy drives on, in its cursed destruction, wreaking this wicked poem.

Poem 26 *2012/9/25.*

Birthright[113] Esau[114]

> "To protect their bloody rite from criticism, Jewish activists have managed to normalise it in England and North America from the 1840s to the 1960s, under fraudulent medical reasons—an amazing demonstration of their power over Christian civilization." —Laurent Guyénot

> "Many wide-spread customs in America, such as giving newborn children Judaic names, or administering circumcision to young newborn males, come from Jewish heritage." —Sunic

Goy, christliche (*moshiach* worship of a Jew), and non-Semitic I was born

And they put my cock to the knife.[115]

As a baby. When I could not say no.

---

[113] Birthright Israel: Anyone of who can prove the purity of their *jüdische* race, anywhere on earth can get free automatic citizenship in Israel. —But anybody who cannot prove they are of pure Jewish race cannot ever become a citizen of Israel —not even if they were born there & all their ancestors lived in Jerusalem for thousands of years. —No "right of return" for native born Palestinians —it is taboo to even be spoken, written or thought.

[114] Political agenda of the ancient *Torah* writer, written & taught as true: *Esau* (Jacob means "usurper")

[115] Unbeknownst to the rest of the world & unbeknownst to most Americans, 98% of American non-Jews have been circumcised in America for the past *110* years.

The head,

Down through the hierarchy, and the *sabbath-goy*,

To the authority figure,

Told my father what to think so he thought it (the authoritarian personality) : [116]

Circumcise (*brit milah*).[117] From a baby

I walked the world hiding the mutilation, unwhole (but not even knowing it).

While uncut-up Europe folks swam in lakes in groups in the nude.

Living,

Thinking I was free ; ignorant.

But the body cut off can not be free of it.

Circumcision was not my race *racines* nor religion, that I came from.

But the tribe of circumcision

Was already the master of the reality frame,

The *intelligentsia*,

Even of *medicina* (*brit milah*),

In the political landscape of the domain

Where

I was born into

As an innocent babe. ...And he far be it knew. And no one told him. Even as adult.

So symbolic, so systemic, of it all ; and the way it all is.

In Greko baths times, *Juden* were embarrassed to be cut-up and found out

So they tried to do mechanical procedures to look uncut-up in the Hellenic era gymnasium.

(And had to "drop their drawers" during East Europe retaliatory *pogroms*, to be found out.)

Whereas, in my day, non-Jew *goyim* parents are all told to cut-up their sons

So they will not be embarrassed to look uncut-up.

"Too bad for you," what's "good for the Jews."

> "Every time a circumcised man looks at his penis, he should see a sign of Jewish power carved into his own flesh before he was even self-conscious." —Greg Johnson

Poem 27 *2012/8/18.*
Egoist 'Dear John Letter'[118]
"It's not you it's me" : I writes,

"I'm not as nice as I want to be. I want to be so nice that I hurt nobody.

But I do not have as much honour as I think I have. I am not as righteous as I think I am.

In the clinch, I try to get my take

and try to think I am not.

And I know. And I do it anyway.

I am not as nice as I thought I was. I am bad. And I can harm. To get what I want.

And I hate it. I don't ever want to harm."

— ... Don't want to harm. For one self-servish reason. —Because my engrammic memories

---

[116] cargo cult: *Mondo Cane*, *Dieu est américain*

[117] male genital mutilation ['*Brit mila*' means 'word covenant'—is Jewish word for circumcision (circle-cut in Latin).]

[118] A "dear John letter" always says, "It's not you. It's *me*."

autistically brood and replay and shame my wrongs over and over until I die. *I* don't want that.

Poem 28 *2012/10/4.*

Scoring

Scoring on women. It has to be said : a man can only score with a woman once!

A man can fuck a woman a thousand times on a thousand occasions

But he only gets *one* score.

A man can fuck a woman for only a few seconds on only one occasion

But he still gets the same one score. One score *per* woman.

You see, men are not interested in the sex.[119] Men are only interested in the scoring.

Men have no serious interest in the sex ;

The sex cannot get a relationship from a man.

Foolish women's *ego* got it wrong :

Men do not, "just want sex" ;

Men, just want to score. Scoring is

"The name of the game." And if man needs sex, he can masturbate.

"Men only want one thing." —"All men are the same."

Poem 29 *2012/10/4.*

La Femme : **A Field Report**

Said to a well young girlfriend, "Why did you go have sex with me that first time?"

Said from the girlfriend, "I figured I would go see how big your cock was. My last boyfriend had a small cock."

Said to the girlfriend, "What do you look for in a relationship? ...What is the most important thing for you in a relationship?"

Said from the girlfriend, "I look for a boyfriend who is good at sex. ...Good sex is the most important thing for me in a relationship."

Said to the girlfriend, "What does good sex mean?"

Said from the girlfriend, "[Serious gaze.] For me good sex means a big cock." … "Even if he was rich, it would not be enough, if he had a small cock."

Said to the girlfriend, "What to you think about the men in your country?"

Said from the girlfriend, "Boys in my country like to use us for sex—and we like it when they use us for sex."

Said to the girlfriend, "What do you want me to do?" (sexually)

Said from the girlfriend, "Just use me. You don't use me."

Said to the girlfriend, "What do you want in life?"

Said from the girlfriend, "I just want a man who cares about me. And loves me."

Said to the girlfriend, "Nice?"

Said from the girlfriend, "[Look of contempt.] For what! Nice, for what?"

Said to the girlfriend, "What are your hobbies?"

---

[119] "The normal fuck by a normal man is taken to be an act of invasion and ownership undertaken in a mode of predation…" —Andrea Dworkin, *Intercourse*

Said from the girlfriend, "I like to look at magazine pictures of famous people."
Postscript : A couple years later, I saw she was fuck-buddying some "African-American"
mulatto in post-European Europe.

"There are only two kinds of women. Angels and sluts. And angels don't exist." —Italiano proverb

"When you eat a lot of sausages, you get tired of eating sausages." —Russ women proverb

"Bachelors know more about women than married men; if they didn't they'd be married too." —Mencken

Poem 30 *2012/10/17.*
Gimme Some Real
Books is not the real,[120] movies and Arts is not the real, and chatting and visiting is not the
real ; and playing faces, not the real.
Talking about this and that, is not the real.
The only real is
The you and me, face to face,
Right now. That is the real. The only real.
The real is you and me touching : breaking
Through the psychological barrier : talking
True and straight and open : creating
Through action and experience and expression.
That is the real. —The "instant *karma.* " [121]
Opening up
Is the real.
Love is the real and
Her analogue,[122] action, is the real.
Real is what is interesting. I only want what is interesting—give me some real.
All I want is some real, just gimme some real.

Poem 31 *2012/10/25.* And *2017/08/22. Luxemburg.*
The Perennial Remains the Same (Bipolar Psychosis): from the Apeiron[123] to the Wotan
"One, who is not, we see: but one, whom we see not, is: / Surely this is not that: but that
is assuredly this." —Swinburne, "The Higher Pantheism in a Nutshell"

"I believe that the centre is a function, not a being—a reality, but a function." —*Derrida*

The *arché* One is storming and raging, behind *the veil of māyā.*[124]
The one is churning and spinning and pouring, and [125]
Twisting, full force, bright, *Agni* fluid fire, behind the veil.
The one is right there in front, behind the veil. Showering out Plato's objects,[126]

---

[120] ontic
[121] *Instant Karma*, John Lennon
[122] *Love And Power*, Rosenfels
[123] wikipedia.org/wiki/Apeiron_(cosmology)
[124] wikipedia.org/wiki/Maya_(illusion)
[125] Yggdrasil/Tree of Life/*Óðinn*/runes/world axis *mundi*: counter-currents.com/2011/04/what-god-did-odin-worship
[126] fiery Muspelheim: viking-mythology.com/theCreation.php

The paradise, the dimension of god,
Right there in front of you, right now, behind the veil.
All things come together, into a snaking Irminsul[127] world-tree pillar, behind the veil.

You are *the be-all and the end-all*[128] of the world ;
Everything that ever will be and has been ;
Everything that is and was.
You are it (*Tat Tvam Asi*) ; you are the man ; the man in the chair, behind the veil.

All things come together.[129] From the One comes the many. "...all the forms of the tree [world]" (*Upanishads*)

Your I's world *versus* the Other I's world.[130]
Putting your world up over their world—a no to the Others' is a yeah to yours—by not lying.[131]
And then the soul releases into itself, self-confidence. Behind the re-velation.[132]

· · · · ·

To wit, Wōtan's *Hávamál* quest for the runes :
There was a time and there was a place.
There was a there that was.
There was a he that cried.
There was a cry and there was a loss of all that was who he was.
There he died ; and there he woke up to the force from where he came.
There he was sucked down and there the he found the vision of, the One of all, to be.
And there he remembered (Mímir's Well) and was born again. And there he woke up alive.
And there he was, more than the he that died.
Ecstatic to be there in that perfect hierarchical chain-of-events Yggdrasil tree that brought all-things here to be.
There was only one man who cracked the code—there was only one man who cracked himself. "When justice is crushed, when evil rules supreme, then I come. For the protection of the good, for the destruction of the evil-doers, for the sake of firmly establishing righteousness, I am born in age after age." (*Bhagavad-Gita*)

> "To the Ancient Egyptians, the Tree of Life represented the hierarchical chain of events that brought everything into existence."

> Diogenes Laërtius summing up Heraclitus's philosophy: "All things come into being by conflict of opposites, and the sum of things (τὰ ὅλα, ta hola, 'the whole') flows like a stream."

Poem 32 *2012/10/31.*

---

[127] Aryaman-pole
[128] *Macbeth*
[129] wikipedia.org/wiki/Unity_of_opposites
[130] Odin/the hanged man tarot card/sacrifice, inversion of good bad: norse-mythology.org/tales/odins-discovery-of-the-runes
[131] wikipedia.org/wiki/Monomyth
[132] re-velation (*i.e.*, unveiling) — revaluation

Nested Plots[133] or Tales within Tales

> *Matryoshka* (Russian doll) is a doll with smaller and smaller dolls nested inside of it.

He liked this doll, even though he barely knew her.

She was interesting and she was hot (*Blauäugige Frau*)—42 kilos.

> But

He was in *Slawischsprachiges Europa* and he

Met her on the internet and she wrote some prostitute-like hints.

Anyway, it was late October. It was their second meeting. He managed to bang her.

It was good.

Touching a woman's cervix with your dick. —Now *that* is fulfilment.

She dressed and said she needed a vocabulary book to use now.

His emotions tensed ; he was hoping she was

> Not going to do this…

He controlled it and remained calm and friendly and gave her his computer to use to write him her message.

As she typed—it took a long time because he did not have a Cyrillic keyboard—he worked to force himself to wait until she was done and to not think.

To blank out the pain of the wait, suspense, destiny.

Her message said : "we are autumn"

"What does that mean?"

He was thinking to himself, does that mean destruction?

He said he did not understand.

She said autumn means beautiful.

He, his being still, still said he did not understand.

He did not understand ; his mind was still racing.

But his fighting mind was relieved that it must, it seems, not mean something fatal.

Then he walked her to her bus.

All okay, for the moment.

Several days later, he realised she was being poetic and it

Was a really cool thing to say. And they continued to meet several times.

…You see, the whole time she was typing it,

he had been 95% sure she would write, "you must pay me money for the sex now."

And that was the big downer he was hoping, vigorously hoping, pushing, a "no" to.

…But, then, a month later, she did complete the fractal and ask for money, and told him she wanted to be, only, a paid-mistress ;

She had only been entertaining some faint notions of heart, which was a "not" to be.

. . . . .

---

[133] —is a doll inside a larger doll inside a larger doll… —A fractal, isomorphic. A story nested inside another story. Recursive - *i.e.* nested structures. —A nested hierarchy set. …Narratives are descriptions about how to go from point A to point B. And within the structure of such myths can commonly be found the common literary "ring structure" chiasmus which uses a series of little symmetrical rings within rings of A'B' opposing binaries. —Setting up the opposite using symmetries of negative-positive antitheses and making up chiasmus crossings to create the good/bad frames and construct the *historia*.

Common interests, compatibility, and
She could feel him when they had sex ; and he could feel her.
Putting on her clothes,
"I'm not going to meet you again."
"Why?"
"Because I am afraid I will fall in love with you."
And, to himself, his facial expression knew at the speed of thought what that meant :
the hypergamy,
The algorithm's iron law,
That he had feared. —He was not high status[134] enough.
No more needed be said.
...And that élite, pretty, doctor woman never did give it to him again. And she was
practically in love with him,
Perfectly, perfectly.

Poem 33 *2012/11/25.*

Women Are to Blame

I blame everything on women. Everything.
Everything is the way it is because of women. (In the lands and times where women are free.)
Women are the choosers. Like Darwin's selection said it, in evolution, women are the choosers.
So everything—life, behaviour—everything, is the way it is because of women.
If you don't like the way life is or you don't like the way men are... if there
Is anything bad or anything that you don't like,
It is because of women. Women are to blame.
Because women are the choosers. It is woman's choice. That is what they select. (Male
Dominance Hierarchies, "patriarchy," form because females use them to select from, quoting
Jordan Peterson. —Women create male hierarchies.)
Men are the way women have made them to be.
Did you hark that? I mean, did you understand[135] that? —Men are
The way women have made them to be. *Cherchez la femme.*
If women only wanted men who wore 5-foot tall, yellow, polka-dot hats,
Then all (*gynocentric*) men would be walking around wearing 5-foot tall, yellow polka-dot
hats ; [136]
because women are the choosers and I blame everything on women. That is what Darwin's
theory of evolution is about.
And I find you, the femininely silent observer, guilty ;
Like women who spread the intolerant religion of Islam into the world by giving their sex[137] to
dusky *Muselmann*, I find you guilty, spreading the seeds of an intolerant religion into the world
; giving birth to a *Sharia* law world is the giving of death to European mankind.

---

[134] *Social Class in America* (*1956*)
[135] etymology: to stand under.
[136] "Males are socialised by the expectations of women." —Charles Murray [aka, Briffault's Law]
[137] "social cheating" strategy so called in evolution

Like crooked white-women who dye their hair black so they can "pass" in their African man's community.[138] I find you guilty.

La femme : selfishly silent and the passive and the pathologically altruistic.

"If civilization had been left in female hands we would still be living in grass huts." —Camille Paglia

Poem 34 *2012/11/26.*

Our Stupid Dreams

"Is a dream a lie if it don't come true, or is it something worse?" (Bruce Springsteen)

I slept a long time to-day so I had a lot of dreams and re-membered them real good.

They were full of wondrous sights and strange activities.

Clear, big, full vision and lots happening. Many big sights and well active.

And they were stupid. Well stupid.

Action, action, action. A wonder if my legs twitched a little bit, like a dreaming dog's does.

It made me realise how truly stupid dreams are.

In them, there is no tragedy, no literature, no philosophy. Not even any good logic.

As stupid as dog dreams are humans'.

It goes to show, there is nothing in there. During sleep the brain-stem just refires neurons left-over from the day about little nouns that you thought about during the day, and uses them to animate your dream with nouns and verbs.

Full of action. Striking action. And chases and stresses and turmoils. Fight-or-flight.

But no tragedy, poetry, or science. As dumb as the dreams of dogs are humans'.

Our dreams are the dreams of chimps ; in high-tech.

This is the revealing thing about dreams. And the

Interesting thing about dreams—how stupid they are.

And now that I am a-wake, I am dreaming to get a new car and a promotion and escape some asshole…

"Flow on to us and make us rich. Drive all our enemies away. O Indu, flow into thy Friend.
Send down the rain from heaven, a stream of opulence from earth. Give us, O Soma, victory in war.
May we obtain thee, Indra's drink, who viewest men and findest light, Gain thee, and progeny and food." *Rg-Veda*

Poem 35 *2012/11/26.*

When Charlie Manson said Musician Thee Not :

"Why do all the pianists play the 300 year old musical scores from Bach, Beethoven, and Mozart, but never their own?

Even if their own would not quite be as good, I am sure they could create a score that was good. It would be their own expression.

Why do all the pretty young rebels, the radicals, the individualists

Playing their guitars on the streets and tunnels

All play the pop songs written by others? Namely the famous.

Why don't the pretty rebels and individualists—these "artists"—sing their own songs?

Un-famous though it may be.

If an artist was fluent at the piano or guitar, an artist would play his own music and sing his

---

[138] Rachel Dolezal, YouTube.com/watch?v=37iNx5YYR_Y

own song. And he would 'sing to god, honour. Not to some fat girl's pussy,' or for money.
...Writers don't write other men's stories. Poets don't write other men's poems.
Why then do musicians only play other men's music? Because
They are only players. Those musicians are not musicians."

Poem 36 *2012/11/26.*
Finding the Voice of the Muse
I talk a lot, chat. So I give to others. So I lose.[139]
But the talking gets it out there. For me to see ; to reverberate.
Language[140] is a tongue. Not a writing.[141]
Talking gives me the muse.[142] I had never realised how interesting what is spoken is.
I found my voice. Does my voice speak[143] to you?

Poem 37 *2012/11/29.*
Ме *Пива* [144]
I found me beer. She is a beer to me.
She is a beer to me brain. She makes me feel like a beer.
Laying with her is a beer to me brain. A beer.
Her body and spirit is like a beer to me. To me brain.
Beer is laying, touching her. I can feel it.
She is beer. She is me beer. Crazy, funny beer.
She makes me feel like drinking a bottle of beer makes me feel.
Beer me body wants, needs, *misses*.
A last desperate attempt of my brain trying to trick me into reproducing.

Poem 38 *2012/12/2.*
Triangulate [145]
The white-hat black-hat dialectic and the dupes.
The game, the contest, the war ; the corruption.
The man-in-black ; the man-in-white ; —the binary. And the patsy dupes—the trinary of the
dialectic. Like how "3-dimensions is the most Parsimonious Model."

The man-in-white says the man-in-black said the dupe is black or says the dupe said the dupe
was black.
The man-in-black says to the man-in-white that the dupe is black.

The man-in-white says the dupe is black to get off on the dupe ; to get over on the dupe.
—For his agenda or to get the man-in-black. And to win favour somewhere and *kudos*.

---

[139] "Even a fool is thought wise if he keeps silent, & discerning if he holds his tongue." —*Proverbs* & *Hávamál*
[140] Language is French for the word tongue.
[141] The proper study of language is spoken speech not written speech, says Chomsky.
[142] wikipedia.org/wiki/Muse
[143] *parole*
[144] Beer (*piva*) in Russian.
[145] discourses.org/OldArticles/Discourse%20and%20manipulation.pdf

The man-in-black says the dupe is black to get off from the man-in-white or to deflect or to exploit. And to win favour.

This is the (forward) propositional fallacy of the man-in-white ; instead of finding a victim and working backwards to find a black.
The white thus creates a black (on the dupe) where none was, maligns, blackens.
Using the man-in-black.
And this word[146]-moral-positional hierarchy of emotional reflexive nonsense is set down and used ; for all manner of undertakings and overtakings.
Two hats
For the same individual immorality. A dialectic giving an excuse for no individual moral responsibility (answer for it).
Mental frames,[147] using the positioning of words, high and low words and positions.
Using fantasy to overtake reality, space (presence).
The man-in-white dupes and lies ; the man-in-black dupes and lies. In a Hegelian dialectic.
As integrity dies ; and the patsy dupes lose.
Until one dupe gets delt-a-strong-hand, says to himself who-you-gonna-believe, and plays-it-weak poker thereby escaping by outing the black-hat in a confirmed lie.
So don't *offer* (info), "don't put it out there."
Interesting that the word "corrupt" means an *unsound* manner.

> "tell not ever an evil man / if misfortunes thee befall, / from such ill friend thou needst never seek / return for thy trustful mind." —*Hávamál*

Poem 39 *2012/12/4.*
Haircut Day
I never know what day it will be. I never plan it.[148]
I just keep myself ready for the moment ; free ; mobile.
Then 1 day I just wake up and pull the trigger ;
—I took my electric-razor and cut off 100% of the hair on my head. Down to the skin.
Ready for battle ; ready for action.
That means to-morrow I take my small bag and go take a train. To a city.
I will live there and do my thing.
No job ; living out of my bankomat.
Because this year is more valuable than the next year ;
Because next year my body will be a year older. And closer to the grave day.[149] And the alternative is nothing.
The time is now. Take it. Use it. See it.
See the show and live in it, on it. And grow.

Poem 40 *2012/12/18.*

---

[146] (*nomos*), Greek for "law" — nomic (name) …norms
[147] wikipedia.org/wiki/Framing_effect_(psychology)
[148] michaelscharf.blogspot.com/2014/02/a-new-equation-for-intelligence-f-t-s.html
[149] Each time a cell divides, the telomeres get shorter. —learn.genetics.utah.edu/content/chromosomes/telomeres

The Character

> *"Ethos anthropoi daimon"* (Man's character is [his] fate) —Heraclitus

I'm not me. I'm only a character ; a psychological character-type.[150]

Thinking and feeling like my type does. Playing it out like my type does.

Thinking I am somebody. Thinking I'm a me, uniquely.

But I am only a character ; only a type.

Sitting here, wondering ; like my type do.

Dealing with my environment ; like my type does ; and does not.

Sitting here trying.

Trying to be me.

Is

Trying to be my character. Trying to grow to be the best that my character can be. Trying and puzzling my whole life long.

Within the parameters of

The character. The character.

Be you mind typed *passiva*, or mind typed *activa*,

Your mind is working like your character-type does.

Me sitting here, or you sitting there,

In a chair. Wondering "what's going on," what is happening, and what to do ...and engrammic "memory scars" galore.

Poem 41 *2012/12/28.*

Don't Say Anything

Make sure you don't say anything.

Poems that make sure they don't say anything, politically incorrect. (Impolitic/ impolite.)

Heavy-metal rock-stars screaming out tough-guy songs, making sure they don't say Anything,

Except for the socially approved, the accepted, catchword angsts and *clichés* and unreal universalisms.[151]

Movies that make sure they don't say anything, about Rome falling, and why. And the big media.

Just the unreal catchword boogies, the blame, and the affirmative unreal universalisms and approved angsts.

And politicians that make dead certain they don't say anything,

About the taboos,

Except for the straw-dog fiscal issues and boogies.

And artists and writers that don't say anything,

No thought taboos,

Except for the accepted. Making sure, making sure, they don't say it. Not a peep.

---

[150] Paul Rosenfels

[151] "Gramsci argued that what led people to discard their native language was the greater prestige of the conqueror's language. The idea of prestige, which had never played a role in classical Marxism, became the key to Gramsci's most famous concept, cultural hegemony." [aka "Social Learning Theory"]

For selfishness and the social-status[152] instinct are deep and high!

Poem 42 *2012/12/30.*

Compute

This relation does not compute.

It does not compute. It does not compute to keep.

It computes to not keep.

All the ugly and sordid and seedy variables. —Ungainly.

It does not compute to keep the relation.

Women should think about all their numerous variables and constraints[153] that they have going for themselves in the equation,

And if it would compute for a computer to keep them.

When does it compute that a man should keep a woman he manages to possess?

So seldom as to be almost never.

For a commit. These girls,

It does not compute to keep them.

Computes—

They say, "why not?" The computer[154] says, "what for?"

It would require a lot of good and quality variables for a relation to compute.

Most girls don't have a chance with the variables they have or what they do with them.

The computer can hope, but when it crunches the data,

To commit, it just does not compute.

And runs away.

Now, where's that article about IVF surrogacy?

Poem 43 *2012/12/30.*

On the Genealogy of Morons

Sometimes I ponder the long line of fools and retards who came before me. My direct forefathers.

And I ponder the long chain of likely fools and retards who could come after me. My descendants. And it makes me bleak. And I ponder how I am probably unique, by happenstance,[155] in this long line. Of fools and retards.

The one only that knew much of what was going on. And the only one that did much different or more than the linear programme that it was already in.

The only microscopic dim bit of Divine Spark amongst a

Bad line

Of fools and retards spanning back, behind me, in an unbroken line, to the origin of life ; and forward past me. Me, one node on this lineage racinate *cours*.

Of fools and retards. This line of mine.

---

[152] *Social Class in America*

[153] wikipedia.org/wiki/Constraint_(information_theory)

[154] wikipedia.org/wiki/Computational_theory_of_mind

[155] *haply*: luck, chance. & *Glück* means happiness in Deutsche.

"Now that light [*Svarga*] which shines above this heaven, higher than all, higher than everything, in the highest world, beyond which there are no other worlds, that is the same light which is within man." —*Chandogya Upanishad* (oldest)

"[Where Brahman-Atman dwells], there are all our true desires, but hidden by what is false. As people who do not know the country, walk again and again over undiscovered gold that is hidden below inside the earth, thus do people live with Brahman and yet do not discover it because they do not seek to discover the true Self in that Brahman dwelling inside them." —*Chandogya Upanishad*

Poem 44　*2013/01/05.*

The Dogs, the Hobos, the Girls

It's better to not get to know them.

Not knowing them personally.

The dogs, the hobos, the girls.

Not watching them dry up and crumble

Over the creeping years

In the darkness and dismay

And blow away.

Not knowing them,

You won't know it

And won't see it. And won't pay for it.

Free from it. Keeping a distance.

Not responsible for it ;

For the dogs, the hobos, the girls ;

Thrown away.

Poem 45　*2013/01/20.*

Outside the Frame

> *"I have often told you stories / About the way / I lived the life of a drifter*
> */ Waiting for the day"* ("Soldier of Fortune", Deep Purple)

I bought a private-room, inside, the first few times I banged her.

Because I was timid.

But after that, I just banged her outside and in isolate toilets.

So I would not have to pay out the money of buying a private-room. A private-room costs 25$.

—It was okay with her. Everything was okay with her.

I tried to take her to church. But I could not find a (private enough) toilet there to bang her in.

After I would give her a cup of instant-coffee in my dorm hostel's kitchen,

I would bang her outside in the darkness in the ice-cold freezing snow at night,

her bending over into the dirty brick wall,

Behind the old hostel building where I would rent a shared dormitory bunk-bed for 7$.

Her standing ; me banging on her back.

So simple. And quick.

—No private-room bed nonsense and stuff from society and movies.

That was a good place, outside, behind that dirty building.

And sometimes in the dirty freezing old stairwell of a dirty apartment building at night, with well lit lightbulb. I like to see.

She was 46.5 kilograms and 19.5 years my junior ;

She was a shy bookworm with glasses. Said to me, "The problem with women is that they get older." And, "I don't want any girl friends. Because she will hurt me more than she helps me."

Her father was a surgeon and she would say was working on a degree in physics.

Waiting for her young French IT engineer boyfriend to soon return from France to live with her again. "A real Frenchman," she claimed (not an Arab).

Then, finally, I banged her against the wall in the freezing, dirty snow, in the darkness, behind my hostel building, (before she walked me to my train)

With my full heavy big backpack on!

My big backpack banging on my back. Bang, bang, bang.

Right before I caught my 11$ train,

To jettison the city.

   "Now I feel I'm growing older / And the songs that I have sung / Echo in the distance / Like the sound / Of a windmill goin' 'round / I guess I'll always be / A soldier of fortune"

Poem 46 *2013/01/23.*

Used Cars

Used.

   Used-up.

Good gone bad.

What is used cannot become unused by changing.

Used is a chronological fact. A history that happened cannot be undone.

But used can fool that it is not used-up.

Getting used is was some choice. Seeking the unused-up is a choice.

Owners choose not the used-up for owning.

Owners go for the unused-up ; not fully deprecated. It is still good.

…The young girlfriend asks, "What are you thinking?"

Poem 47 *2013/01/26.*

Liquid Pure Info

pure info

liquid pure info

give me info

only info

liquid pure info

all I want is info

give it up and give it out

or get out of my world

open the gates of the secrets and the unknown unknowns

and give me your info and keep it flowing

get under me and give up

real

clear

liquid pure data[156]

to me

.

Poem 48 *2013/01/29.*

Futile Thinking

I try to think my culture, country, *la raza* are okay

But they are really not.

I try to think women are okay

But they are really not.

I try to think things are okay

But they are really not.

I try to think a particular woman I know is okay

But she is really not.

The objective world of physical facts

Trumps my wishful thinking.

Thinking away the scab of a cold-sore hiding in the corner of my lip

Does not take it off my skin. No, thinking away her sex-partners

Does not take them off my skin.

And no excuses and thoughts or forgetting can reverse

My act of weakness and my responsibility (answering) for my acts.

Poem 49 *2013/02/22.*

This Guy

"But, you may say, we asked you to speak about man and fiction — "[157]

Who is this guy and what is he doing? What does he think he is doing?

Why is he doing what he is doing? Where does he think he is going?

This guy.

What put him up to this? What put him on this track?

What biology, what biological trick? Drives or driven?

What are his motives? And who all put him up to it?

And all the *wh*'s.[158]

This guy. This guy is you.

Poem 50 *2013/02/25.*

If I Had Feelings

Masculinity can run, but masculinity can't hide, from emptiness, emptiness of feeling ;

It finds masculinity when masculinity is alone,

Masculinity finds masculinity

---

[156] data means give and Sanskrit *datta* means give

[157] Virginia Woolf, *A Room of One's Own*

[158] wikipedia.org/wiki/Interrogative_word

When masculinity is alone
And *nihilismus* finds masculinity.
And or more it finds masculinity when masculinity's body ails and its body falls ill and it feels its mortality ;
That is the moment
When the vanity of the function-pronoun *I* slips down ;
Down enough for masculinity to peer into
Masculinity's emptiness of feeling-fullness, a sickening anguish.
Pang. The empty hole.
And masculinity's aching need to receive love.

· · · · ·

If I had feelings, I would have lots and lots of feelings. Warm, fuzzy feelings.
I would "love you to pieces" with my feelings.
I would have big warm feelings. If I had feelings.
I would feel things and know things. If I had feelings.
Warmth. And I would feel paintings ; and beauty.
I want to know about feelings. Tell me, tell me about feelings.
All I want is feelings.
Your warm, loving, feelings. You worm, spread your warmth.

· · · · ·

All feelings freeze into ice. At the X pole, all is frozen ice,
Snow, barren dry cold air nothingness *nocht* (night).
The nihilating void of feelings. Annihilating my feelings. Empty pit of the heart.
Wanting to find a life of feelings to squeeze and hug and feel.
A puffy pouty feeling to hug.

Poem 51 *2013/03/05.*
Feeling Barely Human
Sometimes, probably when *you* are most right-on, you view out at your environs, moving in it, walking, and you feel barely human.
Barely more than some other animal. Barely different from some category
Framed as not superior in existence (*Dasein*)
And status to that of some other animal.
You feel barely human. Not much selfhood.
And you feel machine-like, in viewpoint, looking out, walking, looking.
Feeling Hofstadter's "the strange loop."[159] Sartre's *Nausea.*

Poem 52 *2013/03/08.*
The Power of Quit : *A Parable of Life*

---

[159] *I Am A Strange Loop*, Hofstadter

Suddenly Johnny was playing with a ball with the other kids.

He would run out and catch the ball

And it dopamine-felt fun to his brain[160] when he caught it.

Suddenly Johnny was older and in higher school

And he was playing on the football team

Practising, training, with the other players.

And he wanted to run out and fetch the ball.

Wanting to dopamine feel fun[161] if he could catch it.

But when it was time to run for the ball

Another player jumped in-front of him.

It was the boy who made the first-rank team.

Johnny was second-rank team.

So he could not run to catch the ball.

When the first-rank boy

Suddenly jumped in-front of him to go for the catch,

Johnny suddenly realised it, what was going on, and turned to the watching coach and Johnny yelled,

"I see."

The coach gave (out) no word. It was not his job

To put-himself-out to say stop. Or to care or to give. His only care was for himself, the coach, to win the game.

Johnny finally saw it.

—Saw that he should have stopped running around a lot, lot earlier.[162]

He had not made the first rank team a long, long time ago.

But he had kept playing on, running around.

The coach never told him to stop. It was not the coach's job to put-himself-out and inform him. The coach was not responsible (answering) for Johnny.

But finally Johnny saw it, that moment, when the other boy went in-front of him, and the coach watched.

Johnny saw that he lost out a long time ago ; but kept playing on ; he saw

That he should have stopped a long time ago.

The coach was, and the other players were, waiting for him to stop.

—Wondering why he kept playing on when he already lost out, a long time ago.

But now Johnny finally saw all that. That moment. He finally caught on.

Saw that he lost out a long time ago and should have stopped running around in circles a long time ago.

And then,

Suddenly, Johnny quit and walked off the field.

　　"When it comes to decision-making, we're all just addled with bias… Being able

---

[160] wikipedia.org/wiki/Dopamine

[161] wikipedia.org/wiki/Operant_conditioning

[162] early: ere, before. nearly

to cut your losses is an incredibly important skill in poker that separates elite players from amateurs." —Duke, *Quit: The Power of Knowing When to Walk Away*

Poem 53 *2013/03/16, Odessa.* Audio: YouTu.be/45h60WDmwjE, SoundCloud.com/programmabilities/the-song-sings

Free of Them All [Set to acoustic-guitar music, Spanish-guitar style.]
Free of them all-l… [163] [Sung, and various chords and *arpeggio*.]
       the song sings [*Spoken*, with 3 fast, strong, full guitar-strums.]
free of them all-l…

free of them all-l…
the song sings [*Spoken*, with 3 fast, strong, full guitar-strums.]
     free of them all-*la-la*. [With 3 fast, strong, full guitar-strums on the all-*la-la*.]

§

Free of them all-l…
   the people [*Spoken*, and various chords and *arpeggio*.]
free of them all-l…

free of them all-l…
   the past
free of them all-*la-la*. [With 3 fast strong full, guitar-strums on the all-*la-la*.]

§

Free of them all-l…
   the lies ["Bridge"—*spoken*, whisper.]
   the scams [*Spoken*, whisper.]
free of them all-l…

free of them all-l…
   the liars
   the ideologues[164]
free of them all-*la-la*. [With 3 fast strong, full, guitar-strums on the all-*la-la*.]

§

Free of them all-l…
   the dreams
free of them all-l…

free of them all-l…
   the lies, the cunning
free of them all-*la-la*. [With 3 fast, strong, full guitar-strums on the all-*la-la*.]

§

Free of them all-l…
   the words
free of them all-l…

---

[163] wikipedia.org/wiki/Negative_Capability
[164] Wikipedia.org /wiki/Ideology —aka "false consciousness" by Marx/Critical Theory.

free of them all-l, free of them all-*la-la*. [With 3 fast, strong, full guitar-strums on the all-*la-la*.]

§

The, song, sings [*Spoken, with 3 fast, strong, full guitar-strums.*]
free of them all-l. ["Bridge"—*spoken*, whisper.]
        free of them all-l. [*Spoken, whisper.*]

The song sings [*Spoken, with 3 fast strong full guitar-strums.*]
free of them all-l.
        free-of-them all-*la-la*. [*Spoken* strongly; with 3 fast, strong, full guitar-strums on the all-*la-la*; and strong quick stop. Then 1 tap on guitar wood.]

> "On this there is this verse: 'When all desires which once entered his heart are undone, then does the mortal become immortal, then he attains *brahman*.'" —*Upanishads*

Poem 54 *2013/03/23. Chişinău, Moldova.*

If Pushkin Was Alive

If Pushkin was alive to-day,
he would sit in a hostel's living-room
sipping a *kawa*
trying to chat with the travellers
the backpackers
marching in and out of the living-room quickly
as they raced in and out past him
to go march off to look at some stupid dead old building of a Pushkin museum.

Poem 55 *2013/04/08.*

Lies, Eating, Consciousness, Conscientious-ness, and Huneker Units

A lot and lots of guys and gals we see
Who are jerks and liars.
But we think to ourselves, "surely they must be a nice-guy like me, in the end."
But, no, actually more close to the facts would be,
That that
Person lying to me and smiling and a jerk,
Would cut my liver out
If he thought he could get away with it and the circumstances were right.
And sometimes a guy thinks he *can* get away with it and the circumstances *are* right.
—And you read about it in the crime news.
Yeah, there are a lot and lots. The low Huneker units[165] guys. The low consciousness[166] guys.
They would cut your liver out and eat it. —Because that is what a lie is doing.

Poem 56 *2013/04/12.*

---

[165] sizes.com/units/huneker.htm
[166] inwit

The Nil
Running and running
From the nil.[167]
Moving and moving, on,
From the nil. The big nil. The big ex.
The *nihil*, can't you see it? Can't you feel it? The zero—"null and void".
Motion, restless motion, is running, away, from being, at, the nil.
The nil is, all that is, is nil.
Motion is moving and running from where the nil is, at.
And the nil is all, everywhere.
Everywhere where motion is not.[168]
So motion keeps moving on,
Up on down the road. To somewhere, somewhere where nil is not.
...Until the motion[169] runs out.[170]

Poem 57 *2013/04/27.*
Holding On
Holding on to the now, here.
Holding on. Here now,
Holding on to it. Holding on to me.
Surviving : my being eating and not my being eaten.
Before I'm dying.
Struggling. For the here and now. The me.
Holding onto my thoughts,
So dim and so clouding. But me,
So holding on,
Now, at, here.[171] Holding on to me, dying.
Consciousness, is this holding on.
Here[172] now, here now, here now…

Poem 58 *2013/04/28.*
The Toll
And She thought she would pull him in with sex.
And he thought he would get some sex for free.

And She thought she would cheat the system and
get the single relationship by doing sex with multiple men.

And he thought he would cheat the system and

---

[167] wiktionary.org/wiki/nil
[168] *ne* | *non* — particles came from Latin *unum* (one); used for negation; later *not*. jstor.org/stable/287766
[169] materialist: everything is 'matter in motion'.
[170] or "luck runs out" — from a viking expression. because your soul is inside you and "runs out".
[171] wikipedia.org/wiki/Indexicality
[172] preposition

get some sex action with no relationship and no relationship worthiness girl.

So they both shook hands and "sealed the deal."

But he was wasting away the precious time-clock of his life and
not getting a quality relationship and not building, but paying the opportunity costs and bugs.

And so was She.

Poem 59 *2013/05/25.*

'May Be' and 'May Not' : quantum particle's what could be and what is
Be what may, everything is maybe.
May-be.[173] May-be not.
May-be yes. May-be no.
May-be on. May-be off.
May-be in. May-be out.
May-be true. May-be false.
Up. Down. Leibniz's 1-0.
May-be. May-be not.
Not not. Not not-not.
May-be. May-be not.
May-be—if…then…
—So may-be or may-be not.
Might.[174] Might not.
No matter what you think or I think ; no matter what you say or I say.
Praxis is governed by be what may ; only the *action* binaries tell.[175] [176]

> Upon learning of these anticipations, Mary Boole recalled her husband feeling
> "as if Leibnitz had come and shaken hands with him across the centuries."

Poem 60 *2013/06/09.*

This Brain of a Mind
This crisp eggshell of a skull.
This fresh orange-peel of a skin. This spongy brain of a mind.
A brain of a mind
Struggles to keep
The focus and the clear
That it had in its bloom. This brain of a mind
Struggles to keep going on
Waxing through its wane. This brain of a mind.

---

[173] essentialism.net/mechanic.htm
[174] 'May' *past participle* is might—might means power. *(macho, macht,* make). …*Be* means to appear, grow…
[175] In economics, this is called a 'revealed preference' –that one's actions show what her true preference is.
[176] wiktionary.org/wiki/tell

Poem 61 *2013/06/17.*
The People Who Do Not Know
Look into the eyes of the faces of the people
Who do not know.
So many of them, the proles, crowds of them,
Who do not know.
The expressions, simple eyes, of the people
Who do not know.
Minds, one level removed
From the real level
Of what moves. So, so easily moved. To think this and to not think that. To obey believe this way and not sub to that way.
Bigot[177] and hypocrite all. And as driven as the horny-goat.
The Great Apes, milling about, here and there.
Look into the eyes of the faces of the people
Who do not know.
Look into the eyes.
 …Just another, nobody know'n noth'n go'n nowhere.

Poem 62 *2013/07/02. Krakow, Poland.*
Our 'Proud Forehead'
> "…in the late *1850*s, physiologist August Franz Mayer identified [shovel-headed] Neanderthal remains from northern Germany as belonging to a Cossack soldier with rickets who had died in *1814* and somehow become buried in 2 metres of fossiliferous deposits."

Always the question : what is wrong with Ukraïna?
Always the answer : it's the corruption,[178] it's the history, it's the economy, it's the culture, it's the government.
But the open-eye can see,
What is wrong with Ukraïna,
Is that too many a man has a shovel-headed slope forehead and thick boney brow-ridge.[179]
That is what is wrong with Ukraïna.
The open eye sees it when it goes just across the border into neighbouring Polska and there in Polska well-nigh[180] all of the *Polacy* have smooth brows and vertical foreheads and life is kind and nice and bright and good there.

Poem 63 *2013/07/04.*
To the Poem Unwritten
The unthought one, of the recursion of thoughts into thoughts.
The unnoticed image, of the looking-glass reflecting into looking-glass infinite.

---

[177] *Bigot* etymology: "by god".
[178] "The meta-analysis of Lynn & Vanhanen (*2012*) shows that national corruption is correlated with national IQ…" edwarddutton.files.wordpress.com/2013/07/intell-928.pdf . Plato's *Republic* said all corruption is caused by *degeneration*.
[179] wikipedia.org/wiki/Neoteny
[180] near, nigh, neighbour

The unspelled out.

Forgotten to the mind and not written. No pencil at hand to snap the photo.

Like a dream forgotten, flitted away.

Or never glimpsed or never lived out. The perspective never attained.

The thought un-cognised. The feeling unfelt or uncasted.

The action unexplained and unsolved. Or never done.

The how-to unworked out and puzzle unsolved. Or words missing the mark.

And word-event never known and experienced.

Leave the world of man weaker and less sentient. Less powerful and less experienced ; and less communicated. More lost.

Poem 64 *2013/07/06.*
The Intellectually Insecure

> The "authoritarian personality"—this term means a person internalises their authority figures—the rich, the elites, the ruling group's grammars—into their identity. —They have a weak ego—their obedience is external to themself.

In the so-called "West," when you are dumb, the big game is,

Play it like you're nice.[181] It will get you far.

Don't know, not sure, and intellectually insecure?[182]

Then play it like you're nice. A nice friendly guy, gets rewarded, and doesn't get punished.

You can't form new analogies—you can't think? Then be the good guy.

Follow the clichéd feelings and beliefs and frames and good-bad high-low perspectives that have been set down for you by your intellectual masters.

The powerful and rich and *intelligentsia*.

And be nice and friendly and polite and politically-correct perspective![183]

That is what works in the West everywhere.

You can't think. But you sure are nice and polite and not low social-status perspective.

And your thoughts obey with a frown[184] when a re-thought (that was set down to be bad low looked-down-upon) is asserted to you. Boo-hoo, for you.

Ask yourself one question, "Who do you believe?"

> "Crimestop means the faculty of stopping short, as though by instinct, at the threshold of any dangerous thought. It includes the power of not grasping analogies, of failing to perceive logical errors, of misunderstanding the simplest arguments if they are inimical to Ingsoc, and of being bored or repelled by any train of thought which is capable of leading in a heretical direction. Crimestop, in short, means protective stupidity." (Orwell, *1984*)

> "The average man never really thinks from end to end of his life. The mental activity of such people is only a mouthing of cliches. What they mistake for thought is simply a repetition of what they have heard. My guess is that well over 80 percent of the human race goes through life without having a single original thought." —H. L. Mencken

> "It is difficult to free fools from the chains they revere." (Voltaire *1694-1778*)

---

[181] "nice" from Latin *nescius* 'ignorant', from *nescire* 'not know'.
[182] "The problem with intellectually insecure whites"
[183] "the bystander effect"
[184] wikipedia.org/wiki/Cultural_hegemony —Gramsci: "Today, the major means…are the mass media."

Poem 65 *2013/07/11. Berlin.*

Berlin's Bullet-Holes

Bullet-holes in churches where European men once had honour (the Deutsch honour, *Ehre,*
comes from the word Arya, Friedrich Schlegel, *1819*).

Modernity's dominators can hid a lot but it can't hide the bullet-holes.

Bullet-holes in the stone walls of the Brandenburg *Tor*. And old building stones.

Most holes are covered up. Fixed.[185]

But it can still be seen. The bullet-holes where aboriginal men fought for *Blut und Ehre.*

In Berlin you see it. In Berlin you see how the city was bombed *platte*

Into submission to extinction ;

Völker und Rassen killed because they were Deutschen ;

Then the victors, the new rulers,

Decided they must have revenge

And ensure that the aborigine will never rise again for its survival.

So the indigenous folk were replaced with replacements.[186] All non-Europid replacements.

Now the place is largely non-Native. With *Muselmann* babies everywhere. The aboriginal
Europids extinct within a few more breeding-cycles.

Politics, "war by other means," is always a genocidal operation.

If Germany won WWII, England, France, and Germany, *etc.*, would be Europeans today.

Who was right? "History is the judge."

Poem 66 *2013/07/14. Berlin.*

Something Sometime Said or Done

A picture is not me. That's not me.

Only I am me—and I am only, right now. This moment.

That picture you are looking at is not me.

Only I am me, right now.

Only *this* is me. *That* image in a picture is not me.

Only me right now is me. So talk to me, right now.

If there was anything to express or something to communicate or something to give or
something to do,

Do it right now. Now is the time.

Looking at a picture of me in the past is not looking at me. Looking at a picture of me in the
future is not looking at me. It is a fake image, only, of me.

Only my *by*, my being of me, is me. And that I is hereby right now.

Photos are not me

---

[185] wikipedia.org/wiki/Victor's_justice

[186] "Renaud Camus said flatly that France is being colonised by Muslim immigrants with the help of the
government & the media. He calls it 'The Great Replacement.' …'The Great Replacement is very simple,' he
explained. 'You have one people, & in the space of a generation, you have a different people.' … Camus accused
the French media of covering up the situation in the name of political correctness, essentially telling the French
that the Islamization they see happening with their own eyes is not happening. … 'Television is saying every day
& school is saying every day that what is happening is not happening, that it is all in your head, that it is an optical illusion,'"

But my word is me.[187] A piece of me—what I say and write.

Listen to me and, even, read me. That is me.

Even a memory of my deed or word is a whit[188] of me, my spirit.

But my picture, that is not me.

Don't take a photo now. Forget the photos of the past. And don't look at photos in the future.

Don't take a photo. And don't paint a picture. —Remember what I spoke, or read my words.

The word, the mental express, and the do

Of some now.

Don't take

My picture—

Give me

Some informed words or do something for me, give to me,

Now. Or take listen to me, now. Now is the time. All else "is for nought."

Poem 67 *2013/07/25. Krakow, Poland.*

Derrida's Particularistic *Différence* [189]

> Spinoza (and Hegel), "*omnis determinatio est negatio.*" Every determination is a negation [of the One].
> Relative to [Spinoza's] One, everything else is determinate, and everything determinate is negation.

To want "positive energy" is to want "negative energy"

Because there is no positive if there is no negative.[190]

To create a positive relief, there must be created a bas-relief.

An affirmative action to one side is a negation action to the Other side.

There is no making good without making bad ; in deed and in word thought.

"As evil cannot exist without the good,"

Most of words—it's all propositions.[191] There is no good. There is no bad. Except points of view of win or lose. Superior or inferior.

Like there is no big or small. Except in relation to something else.

A, "man is the measure," of difference—the *particular*—the Other,

Such is thought—wherein which *logic is always identitarian* as Adorno conceded to

Heidegger ;[192] in the "primate mounting behaviour" of a monkey's cognitions.

> "Without injustices, the name of justice would mean what?" —Heraclitus, *Fragments*

> "The opposite of a true statement is a false statement, but the opposite of a
> profound truth is usually another profound truth." —Niels Bohr

> "If you hear that Caesarea and Jerusalem are both in ruins or that both are flourishing
> peacefully, do not believe it. Believe only a report that Caesarea is in ruins and Jerusalem is
> flourishing or that Jerusalem is in ruins and Caesarea is flourishing." —*Talmud*, Tractate Megilla

---

[187] Heidegger believed language was one of the most important concepts for Dasein: "Language is the house of being, which is propriated by being & pervaded by being."

[188] a tiny amount, bit.

[189] wikipedia.org/wiki/Différance / He got it from "Saussure argues, languages have a relational conception of their elements: words & their meanings are defined by comparing & contrasting their meanings to one another."

[190] wikipedia.org/wiki/Unity_of_opposites

[191] propositions are sentences, in logic

[192] wikipedia.org/wiki/Dominance_hierarchy

Poem 68 *2013/07/26. Krakow, Poland.*

The Poems of My Mind

There's nothing left
but the poems of my mind. Swirling, drifting, dropping
sense and nonsense and sense. Swirling up and replaying
a life lived out
now over and done.
A bizarre history
so awful. Looking back.
Every year was learning, becoming awares, seeing
the human animal was even
more wicked, dishonest, evil [193]
than was beware the year before.
There's nothing left now
but the poems of my mind. Swirling
sense and nonsense. Of a youth, of a life
now finished off and over.
Nothing left
but that *bizarro* history
of losing.
A sordid history
of being lied and used
and losing out
and missing out
and being left out.
It's over now. Looking back.
Nothing left
but the poems of my mind. Swirling sense and nonsense
and, seeing, seeing
the animal Man for what she was, is.

Poem 69 *2013/08/17. On a train, somewhere in Galicia.*

Operation Mindfuck

A girlfriend talks of anal-sex and sex-toys and orgasms and the seedy men who power-fucked her
And she wonders why the man's interest[194] dwindles and he falls away.
And she *proves to herself*, "another man who only wants sex."
And she only chooses for sex, as she thinks to herself that she only "want long-term love and

---

[193] "Individual *versus* group selection results in a mix of altruism & selfishness, of virtue & sin, among the members of a society." "Competing is intense among humans, & within a group, selfish individuals always win. But in contests between groups, groups of altruists always beat groups of selfish individuals."
—brainyquote.com/quotes/authors/e/e_o_wilson.html
[194] evolutionary psychology: "paternity certainty".

a family" ("family values").

And she is alone (no commitment).

As she hypergamous-ly chooses men who she has nothing in-common with and shares no hobbies with and thinks that only her love-lust feelings (triggered by her sex-drive called hypergamy) matters.

And wonders why—no long-term relationship can be.

...As the man realises he should cut down his sex meeting with her from 3-9 times total,

To 1 time only and then escape from her.

Even if she be a 10!

And after he "gets off" on every 1-night-stand, he says to Her, "(sorry) I'm not looking for a girlfriend or sex. I am only looking for a long-term relationship (a wife)." —*The truth.* And says, fare-well, ("goodbye and good riddance.")

Poem 70 *2013/08/24.*

My Religion

In Goth tongue *wot* (god), word, whisper, water/wet, wit are all from the same root.

In the silence there is a chatter
let it come. In the easy moment when the drunken[195] words come word by word string
or half-sleep
the cannabis-like mood. "When *soma* speaks from within you." (*Vedas*)
Give me some words to soothe me. These things—these words—are my poetry
my religion, my salve.
More soothing,
and meaning, and interesting
than new cars and career job and religions.

Word drop by word drop, let them come
Flowing[196] through to me.
Words help and soothe and clear and pure.
Let the word speak
To me.
Words words, grammar-ing together.
Where I can find them.
Word drop by word drop. What will I find?

Word balm spreading. Word balm feeling.
Coming on through.
The *musica* of the sound of text.
Word the balm.
Healing the loneliness of the emptiness of this night.
Word balm spreading. Salving, healing, the warring mind.

---

[195] wikipedia.org/wiki/Mead_of_Poetry
[196] *Fluxion* (the rate of flow) was Newton's word for a function. Fluent: "the flowing."

The dull mind, the dark mind, scared and scarred.
Word balm spreading. The salving text.
The musical soundings. Hark, through the silence and the noise.
Word balm spreading.

Poem 71 *2013/09/09.*

Ex Spotting

I saw an ex, going down the escalator. I was going up, I suddenly saw her, across from me.
She did not see me, because she was patching on some makeup, while looking into her tiny
looking-glass.
I was shocked to see her, across from me. I thought, to yell, hello,
I thought, I ought to. But I did not.
Happy[197] to escape, to rid,
Once again. *Exeunt.*

Poem 72 *2013/10/09.*

My Cuck'd Uncle's Will

> "Grendel's mother, monstrous hell-bride, brooded on her wrongs" —*Beowulf*

Wanting and wanting, lacking and lacking, in the shrinking gyre.
Always left wanting, wanting and wanting, and wanting, to be esteemed.
The self-esteem—wanting the self-estimation
To be high and bigger and higher
—But left wanting. —Lacking. In the shrunken life gyre.
No lovers ; no life ; no action ; no novel.
Only the shrunken gyre of individualistic blood-relations. —That most shrunken of gyres.
That most shrivelled thread of life. (Not the group.)
Shrunken down to his empathless Aspergian-traits sister. Cold-butch sister, at that.
The brother had a shrunken life gyre—wanting and lacking.
He wanted and wanted, to be esteemed, self-esteemed up in estimation, for himself.
So when his butch sister cried out to him on the phone about her young villainous teen son,
he replied, so chivalrously, "Do you want me to come over and kick his ass and beat him up
and kick him out for you."
Wanting and wanting, lacking and lacking.
20 years later he put a gun to his head in a cornfield and blew his brains out—at 69.
He left his little will (ten thousand dollars)—that wanting and wanting will.
His *last will and testament* left everything to that cold butch sister's granddaughter. (Whose
kind, when he looked at, did not appear his or her own). —Some air-head *mulatto* deep
Down South. —His last lineage blood drop—to his esteem, to his blood drop. In the
shrunken gyre. To pander for the last esteem of his shrivelled up old cold-butch sister.
His "last will and testament."
Wanting and wanting, to be the white-knight status, of his little shrunken world.

---

[197] *Hap* means chance, luck.

Wanting to be esteemed, to be estimated to be deemed[198] favourably by his shrivelled up old cold-butch sister.

—By his god-awful, ignorant, cold sister. My mother.

"It could have been me."

...And his newspaper obituary—authored by his refrigerator sister—read : "He is survived by his grand-niece."

> "The factor in infantile autism is the parent's [autistic DNA parent's] wish that
> the child should not exist." ("refrigerator mothers theory", Bettelheim)

Poem 73 *2013/10/10.*

Mind of a Dog [199]

A dog has a home ; it knows where it lives and it knows where it sleeps.

A dog does its job, and it loves what it favours to eat, and it likes to be petted.

A dog knows when it is hot and when it is cold.

A dog knows a dog from a cat.

A dog knows when it is day and when it is night.

A dog plays ball and barks.

Dogs mate.

A dog knows pain and hunger ; and knows fear and obedience ; and aggression ;
and has a tell-tail of many an emotion.

A dog does this and does that, and goes a'round.

Dogs do not know what their masters are doing.[200]

Most people, they are not more than dogs.

Poem 74 *2013/10/13.*

Monkey Times

Yes, there will be a post anthropocene.

Yes, the anthropocentric view is not the overall view like the ecocentric view is.

Yes, man will come to an end, so nothing really matters about man.

Yes, "all is One."

Yes, yes, yes, yes, says the *Bhagavad-Gita*'s Krishna-soul to Arjuna, but

Fight, fight, fight, fight to be-exist and to grow, because that is your nature (Arjuna's "duty"),
and that is the nature.

Fight for in particular you, you'uns, place, culture. To survive and to be better.

Be-cause that is how life's nature and your nature works.

Don't be passive to your death. All men are "already dead" anyway.[201]

Fight on, Arjuna. Raise your war banner with its emblem of the "rampant monkey,"[202]

Yes, this time will only be a finite moment in the *kósmos*. But[203] it was a real time (that

---

[198] deem is Old English for judge

[199] Reference to Bulgakov's "Heart of a Dog".

[200] "No longer do I call you servants, because a servant does not know what his master does," *John 15:15*

[201] famous line from the *Bhagavad Gita*.

[202] In the *Bhagavad Gita*, the emblem on the war flag of Arjuna is that of a "rampant monkey".

[203] thefreedictionary.com/adversative

happened), forever, nonetheless.
To action. Fight on! You monkey in the field.

Poem 75 *2013/10/23.*
You Don't Exist
    "Only the rich can afford the luxury of not having a homeland." —Ramiro Ledesma Ramos

You don't exist. You don't count.
You don't have a community. You don't have a tribe. You don't have a union, a solidarity.
So you don't exist. You don't count. You don't matter, materially.
You don't get help. You don't get-the-goods.
You don't have an identity. You don't have a group. You don't have a tribe.
Now you don't have a country ; you don't have a homeland.
You don't exist. You don't count.
You don't have power. You don't get-the-goods.
You're not the votes. You don't count.
You're not a woman with a bastard baby.
   —You don't get the healthcare and welfare and housing.
You're not the votes. You don't count.
So you don't exist. (As language linguistics is spatial logic.)[204]
Now go "work and pay taxes" and die.
Don't I get to be smart? —Don't I get to be a person?

Poem 76 *2013/10/30.*
America Caused the *Holodomor* : A Grand Narrative
Thoughts are ion[205] event-driven chains of synapses.
And logic is a chain.[206] A chain of true/false events. A "line of reasoning"—reasoning is "what follows from what." Logic means "if-then" (antecedent and consequent). And science reasoning is a chain—"the knowledge of consequences, and dependence of one fact upon another," wrote Hobbes.
And history is a chain. A chain of events. That betide because of *priori* events.
And written-history[207] is a fictional and/or factual chain ; a construction.

In really, America caused the *Holodomor*. ...Because history is a chain. A chain of events. And logic is a chain.

When the "Judeo-Bolsheviks" killed the *tzar* and became the new czar (revolutions are nothing but the replacement of one group's elites with another group's elites, "the circulation of elites theory"), a new state called Ukraïna was struggling to exist as a state independent. Struggling

---

[204] conferences.inf.ed.ac.uk/cogsci2001/pdf-files/0845.pdf
[205] bris.ac.uk/synaptic/basics/basics-2.html
[206] "2.03 In the atomic fact objects hang one in another, like the members of a chain." —Wittgenstein
[207] Thematic Relations Hypothesis: "In any semantic field of [EVENTS] & [STATES], the principal event-, state-, path- & place-functions are a subset of those used for the analysis of spatial location & motion" [Gruber]

with Russia.[208] That is why, earlier, when WWI started, Ukraïna was allies with Deutschland. Deutschland/Ukraïna fought the AntiFa—England, France, and Russia. Deutschland/Ukraïna would not have lost WWI. They only lost for one reason. Because U.S.A. joined England-France-Russia AntiFa and gave them all the money and resources and U.S.A. soldiers so that they could defeat Deutschland/Ukraïna. Deutschland/Ukraïna lost because of the U.S.A.. (America entered WWI, as the *Balfour Declaration* shows, because England Jewry networked to get the U.S.A. to enter it for England. *In exchange* for England Jewry and American Jewry winning the U.S.A. entry into England's war, international Jewry won rights[209] to Palestine from England.) After WWI, Ukraïna was the loser and was weak. This allowed the new Judeo-Bolshevik regime in Moscow to come in and dominate Ukraïna. —And this "Russia" (the language and country were first named "Russia" by Peter the Great) logically wanted to punish Ukraïna for fighting against them in WWI (and deter it). (And, may-be, the "Judeo-Bolshevik" commissars wanted revenge/prevention for the Cossack pogroms on the *Ashkenazim* for hundreds of years back.) So, Russia made a deliberate programme to exterminate the Ukraïner—the Cossacks. They conducted the *Holodomor* (famine) for 2 times over the next 10 years. This exterminated 7 million Ukraïner. (Thusly, later, Barbarossa Op. was greeted as liberators from the Rusky *"Weltfeind - der Bolschewismus"* oppressors.) —Then Ukraïna was more safely incorporated into the U.S.S.R. (Moscow). …History is a chain. Ukraïna only lost WWI because of the U.S.A.. This event directly led to Ukraïna being hit with genocide by the "Judeo-Bolsheviks"[210] running Russia in the guise of the U.S.S.R. out of Moscow. History, logic, is a chain—a chain of events. Therefore (heretofore) America caused the *Holodomor*.

Everything is the way it has to be, because everything is connected. So everything is perfect. Because everything is the way it has to be.

Why did Russia give up its old pretext of annexing their neighbours to promote Communism and now they just annex their neighbours to "liberate" lands from "nationalism/Nazism"?[211] Communism provided a universalist, ideological justification that sounded progressive and internationalist at the time, especially to left-leaning Liberals in the West and the Third World. It simply swapped one legitimising story for another once the old one lost all credibility.

Poem 77 *2013/10/31.*
'Ugly Cow'
An old woman got on her metro train to-day
And sat across from me. She had a big bouquet of wildflowers
Clutched in her two fists
Holding them to her chest. Taking them home. "Grinning with self satisfaction."

---

[208] counter-currents.com/2014/03/white-nationalist-delusions-about-russia
[209] Hohfeldian analysis: ics.uci.edu/~alspaugh/cls/shr/hohfeld.html
[210] *Żydokomuna*
[211] The English word Nazi came from Yiddish word *natsy* for German word *National*. Yiddish word for a National Socialist party member is *natsi* (plural: *natsis*). National Socialists disliked being called this Yiddish word.t The term was popularised by Jewish intellectuals and the international *Presse* which they owned in America.

Very beautiful wildflowers. An assortment.
The crone[212] saw them growing in the wild. And she had to go over and cut them down and kill them
And take them. With the unthinking greed of a cow.
The rare wild seeds of beauty lost for-ever.

Poem 78 *2013/10/31. metro Klovska*
Ich Bin [213]
I love the roses in the Spring
when they smell
soft wet and rosy.   Words they are to me[214]
when I see them and touch them
and pick them
and as they die they are forgotten.

· · · · ·

All things are seen as words—every object has a bunch.
If men need to give women bouquets of flowers, it means those men are short of words ; so they give bouquets of flowers.
So I don't need to give you flowers ; for I have a plenty of words.

· · · · ·

In the air, and in the tune of the man playing the violin in the tunnel crosswalk. In the routine sights of "the daily grind." In the seeing and in the shops and in the objects and in the trifle.
I see in and I move in and I breath in.
And it brings in the words of the day, as I walk and see and thought.
The words and sights, in the air.
In the berries in the cup, that I bought, in the shop, ere the tunnel crosswalk, in the air.
I am in them. In the berries in the cup. I am in them.
In the air and in my step. In the berries in the cup in the sights in the words in the moods in the air. As I walk and see and word, in the air—in it all.

Poem 79 *2013/10/31.*
'What's What'
There's something there, where nothing is.
It makes what is ; and what isn't, it wasn't.
And it's in the man who is at one with himself.
It's in the little boy who won't eat his peas.
It's in the rebel who says, "No."
It's the Mind in the forehead

---

[212] French *charoine*, meaning dead flesh.
[213] wiktionary.org/wiki/*ich*. And Heidegger notes that *bin* means been (be) or, specifically, "dwelling" (building).
[214] *me* is a dative: logolalia.com/arspoetica/archives/003102.html

That draws on its neurons.

It's when all that we have (left) is what's in us.

Poem 80 *2013/10/31.*

Text Photo [215]

> "A picture can never be as explicit as a sentence." —Michael Dummett

Thereby hangs a robe.

I hung it up. Now it's hanging down.

Falling down are cotton rolls of towelled fabric.

Chequered—falling down. Hanging up.

What hangs up, must hang down.

> "The road up and the road down are one and the same." —Heraclitus

Poem 81 *2013/10/31.*

'Don't Mind if I Do'

> "He who advances conquers; he who hesitates is lost." —Bertrand du Guesclin

When the action is on,

> Don't have a dream and don't have a thought ;
> Don't have a wish to go for.

Just take what is in the offing

And see what turns out.

> Don't have a dream and don't have a thought ;
> Don't have a wish to go for.

It will spoil your actions

And you'll lose out on the action.

When the action is on,

> Don't have a dream and don't have a thought ;
> Don't have a wish to go for.

Poem 82 *2013/11/09.*

Spatiality

Coffee rounds the cup. Spoon plunges into it.

Cloudy coffee reflecting the window's sky.

Everything I see is spatial.

And all that I think is spatial.

And moving[216] in the spatial.

Locating with logic or dotage.[217]

Organising the space.[218]

---

[215] 'Language is a picture of the world. (For a picture to depict it uses **logical form** - the form of reality.)' —para. Wittgenstein

[216] wikipedia.org/wiki/Fictive_motion: Leonard Talmy

[217] "spaced out"

[218] grid cells ncbi.nlm.nih.gov/pmc/articles/PMC5248972/

With binary oppositions of on it or off it.[219]

Or timeline,[220] where "Time is the measure of movement. ([Aristotle])" Or numberline, where maths defines number as scalars and vectors. Or quality springing from measure of quantity. [221]

Or truth is, when, compared, "laid against reality like a measure" spoke Wittgenstein. Or points[222] of view. Or categorising in on a class or not in on a class. Or metaphors of is at's. Or nouns, designating bounded regions within abstract constructs which are devised to track their passage.

From prepositions to propositions to all of language. From *from* to *to*.

Cognito positioning in space.

As does the fly's and the mouse's.[223]

Poem 83   *2013/11/09.*

Oy on an Impoverished Youth

My fingers are dancing over the piano keyboard in my mind.

Crashing in thunderstorms of keys and tunes. And tapping around slowly then quickly.

The high keys are so clear in their taps. The low blend into crashes.

Using all the keys to every extreme ; floating around naturally. From delicate *pianissimo* to powerful *fortissimo*.

Oy how to harness the mind, and manifest it, play it? *Oy* how to compose it, read it, and do it?

> "Show me a man who is good at billiards, and I will show you a man with a wasted youth." —Wordsworth

Poem 84   *2013/11/09.*   Kyiv, metro Obolon.

'This Mortal Coil'[224] of Thrownness[225]

"O Fortuna…" You ran me out and you ran me off and you ran me back again.

You ran my path and you ran my mind and you ran the world.

And at story and story I saw many a thing to see.

And I saw vision and I saw sight that should never have been.

I tried it all and all I tried left me with nothing at all.

Come my desire came my will and come my doubt came my judgement.[226]

And here I am with a loss in my pride and a nothing left but lose.

So I am wondering why and seeing how I was lost at birth in life.

Until no more left no more run to ruin by *you* "this mortal coil" dubbed *rota fortunae* of life.

---

[219] Derrida says meaning in the West is defined in terms of binary oppositions, "a violent hierarchy" where "one of the two terms governs the other." wikipedia.org/wiki/Binary_opposition

[220] etymology of *time* means "to stretch"

[221] "One important dialectical principle for Hegel is the transition from quantity to quality, which he terms the Measure. The measure is the qualitative quantum, the quantum is the existence of quantity."

[222] "2.0131 A spatial object must lie in infinite space. (A point in space is a place for an argument.)" —Wittgenstein

[223] Sensory-motor circuitry used by animals appears to have been re-purposed (that is, "exapted") for use in thought and language by human beings. —Lakoff

[224] wikipedia.org/wiki/To_be,_or_not_to_be, *Hamlet*: "this mortal coil"

[225] Heidegger's *Geworfenheit* (thrownness); and for Heiddegger "facticity" is the particulars of your thrownness. Heiddegger's concept of "thrownness" is that we do not create our identities. our identities are handed to us.

[226] Hobbes

"I saught my death, and founde it in my wombe" —"Tichborne's Elegy"

"For as you began, so you will remain," —Hölderlin

"'Dost thou know, [,,,], that puller (ruler) within who from within pulls (rules) this world and the other world and all beings?' [...] 'He [...] who knows that thread and him who pulls (it) from within, he knows *brahman*, he knows the worlds, he knows the *devas*, he knows the Vedas, he knows the *bhutas* (creatures), he knows the Self, he knows everything.'" —*Upanishads*

[*Karma* (Sanskrit), *wyrd* (Teutonic), *dán* (Celtic), and *Moreia* (Hellenic). Many Greek tragedies, such as Oedipus, are based on this idea which is personified in Greek mythology by the *Moreia* (the Fates) who create the "thread" of a person's fate, measure it, and cut it at death.]

Poem 85 *2013/11/10.*

Örlög : **It All Matters**

"The office does not forgive, the past cannot be returned." —Putin

All of the tear all of the destroy all of the loss,
All of the lie betray trick double-cross treason[227] con broke-word,
All of it,
As wickedly brilliant Jewry says, "it cannot be forgiven."[228]
No. What was taken from you can not be fore-given to[229] back *by you.*[230]
It is lost. It is sealed in space time's matter as "a done deed."
For-ever in the present. Because all events are interconnected and the sins go to the Winner's spoils and on to her eggs then seeds. Growing exponentially[231] on into the future.
Just as your losses grow exponentially on the loss side of the ledger of what was lost.
Yes, all is interconnected. So there is no forgiveness. (It is immaterial.)
In really, nothing is forgotten. —It all matters.[232] That is why the scales of Justice measure weights.
So don't, put a judgement over your doubt with a forgive wish, as Hobbes[233] might word it.
Don't even forget.
Don't except it. Just accept it. Take it. Take responsibility[234] (answering) for it.
Going forward : past it.
Getting over it : putting it behind you. Farther and farther away.

Poem 86 *2013/11/10.*

Words, Points of View, Frames

After a man and a woman fuck, it is the woman who wants to meet a second time. Not the man.
This means it is the woman who "only wants sex." Not the man.
The man does not want sex : he does not want to meet a second time.

---

[227] *treason* in Latin: "to hand over"
[228] Never forgive, never forget, says jewry. An eye for an eye, a tooth for a tooth, says Jehovism.
[229] "Forgive" always has an implied "to" —because forgive takes the dative case.
[230] remunerative (re- "back" + *munerari* "to give")
[231] exponent: also called *power laws* or scalable laws. The power is the number of the exponent.
[232] material-dialectic: "everything is atoms in motion".
[233] Hobbes says desire makes our will while doubt makes our judgement.
[234] etymology: message

When the man only wants sex, he also will meet a second time. Like a woman who only wants sex.

No. Men do not only want sex.

That is why they only want to fuck a woman one time and then get away from her.

And keep the dream alive

Of finding

A worthy and compatible mate. Not sex.

Poem 87 *2013/11/11.*

Indifference[235] Linguistics

Did you ever want to possess something? Did you ever not want to possess something? Did you ever possess something?

If possess is an addition, then want to possess is a subtraction.[236]

So not want to possess is the only way to avoid a subtraction.[237]

It is the only way to avoid anger.[238] After being taken by lies.

· · · · ·

What you have, you do not want.

What you want, you do not have.

—As the form of material reality forms the language, we obey the sentences.[239]

So we suffer, in thought.

And while the Dawkin "meme" virus of words[240] lives in our human bodies, humans are what words use to replicate themselves.

Poem 88 *2013/11/11.*

Tangle

In the words I've woven of my world, my life, myself, my story, my point of view, my context, my truth, my web of *wyrd*, is there a tangle? [241]

Have I missed something? Was one word off in the sequence? [242]

What doubts were outs that I used as judgments? [243]

Where is the tangle in the fabric of my life? My textile of text.

How to find a tangle?

And where will I find the words of wisdom that will untangle it? I wonder ; and peer from outside angles.

Poem 89 *2013/11/12.*

---

[235] wikipedia.org/wiki/Indifference_curve
[236] *if...then* is a *modus ponens*. wikipedia.org/wiki/*Modus_ponens*
[237] Hobbes says all math can be reduced to addition & subtraction.
[238] see Rosenfels on anger
[239] wikipedia.org/wiki/Triangle_of_reference
[240] William Burroughs wrote that words are a virus in man's body.   wikipedia.org/wiki/Memetics
[241] Contradiction, Law of noncontradiction, Square of Opposition.
[242] "Hobbes defined truth as consisting in *the right ordering of names in our affirmations*;"
[243] Hobbes

Flat

There stares blank walls and hard edges.

There looks concrete paint.

There burns electric light-bulb.

There lays ragged chair and messy bed.

There sounds background noises.

There puffs dead air.

There's a crack-up in the ceiling.[244]

There stares blank.

There is me.

Poem 90 *2013/11/25.*

New Man Old

I follow the sun, I follow the path, I follow the speak, and I follow the things.

I've seen more real evil than any imagination could dream up, and I've seen less real love than one average Hollywood movie concocts.

I see what is and what always has been.

Through the same eyes from the past man, though not through eyes of the past man.

I am free from the gods and the scams of yore.

I see a new world, through the eye-opener of science's more knowledge.[245]

Yes, I am the same man : the same man from old.

Though[246] I am a new man : the new man of old.

· · · · ·

God in my soul, I feel, is the *Mannus*, in my soul, I feel.

The deep, in my voice, I feel, the weight, in the speak, I feel, the Lord, in my soul, I feel, is me.

The me, that has been 'round, even, before me has been around.

He makes do, the best he can, with the what's, he does not have.

And, he tries, the best he can, to be more, right and free. Around.

And, he tries, the best he can, to grow, more, than he is now.

And, get done on, more. Around.

That's him, who you feel hear *Sprechen*,

And, that's, what he, is doing there,

And, that's why he's even there. The *Geist*-in-the-machine aspect. Sentient intentionality.[247]

Poem 91 *2013/11/25.*

Wind Eye [248]

I see the stars in the lights to-night. —The apartment-block windows outside my window.

Outside my window, I see the city. I see the edges, through the streets.

---

[244] The Kinks

[245] a kenning

[246] english-for-students.com/Concessive-Clauses.html

[247] wikipedia.org/wiki/Intentionality

[248] etymology of window

I see the far away, *panorama* slice. I see the garbage dumpsters, up close.
I see the dark windows, of the city, outside my,
Little window, my poor-man's window.
I see the dark cold night, of the city,
Where I am at.
I'm at here. At my little poor window, on this little angle, into a slice, of a corner, of the city.
The big dark cold city, to-night.
My poor little window.

Poem 92 *2013/11/27.*
Being New Things
Being new things.
Not the same old.
Not the same old wage-slave.
Getting out of the same old cube.
Being new things.
Out from under the thumb of hierarchic submissive *autonoma*.
Not the same old personality and modes of doing, thinking.
Being new things.
Not[249] the same old city and state.
Not the same old title and status.
Being new things.
Dying the old lives out.
Being new things.
Taking new mind-space.[250]
Heightening vantage points on the petty.
Seeing more of the big picture—being less stupid.
Emancipation.

Poem 93 *2014/01/17.*
Birds Fly Dropping Down
Birds fly. Birds fly. (Off their cables.)
Dropping down. Dropping down. (For energy conservation.)
Birds fly dropping down.
Birds fly. Dropping down.
If you give, you will suffer. If you help, you will get hurt.
No initiative goes unpunished, observes the old Rúss proverb.
And you do it ; and you try ; you speak up.
And the punishment pangs you so you drop it.
Dropping down. Dropping down.

       "A wise man holds his tongue. Only a fool blurts out everything he

---

[249] negation & modal verb.
[250] wikipedia.org/wiki/Mental_space if-then: *space builder* "then".

knows; that only leads to sorrow and trouble." (*Proverbs* 10:14)

Poem 94   *2014/01/29.*

Choking the Neck of Love

A new place, a new name, a new life.

Moving towards, moving aways.

Choking the neck of love.

And "it pains me to do it."

A new place, a new woman.

Choking the neck of love.

Looking out the bus windowpane,

Watching the countryside of objects go by. The smooth glassy sheen of the nightscape.

Realising it is me out there I see. Out there is in my head. Held there and mapping—

Finding a new place

To choke the neck of love.

Poem 95   *2014/02/15.*

Counting Electric Sheep [251]

Nightfall dropped down ; that singular curtain dropped, with a striking ugliness, like a

tatar-eye's singular eyelid. And

As my brain rests in its case, I feel. The slumber that is coming on, to relieve me from my

feel. And

Rest my god-awful thoughts, of blood and vile and defection and treachery and death. And

Genes are but proteins (with replicating RNA), but protein (the gene) is not alive. And

Atoms' electrons come from Nothing.[252] And

Nothing (in particular) doesn't exist, because Nothing is a universal and Fregian universals,

logically, aren't existential (don't exist). And

All the atoms in my body were created by exploding stars' deaths. And

Colours (*qualia*) don't exist.[253] And

Here I lay and live and die.

Eternal oblivion before I was born : then born and lived : then eternal oblivion again at death.

Sleep,[254] dreams, take me away…

As I think what is was

And as I think what is was not.

Canting, "In the sweetness of the darkness I can sleep."

Oh night embers of the starry sky, the next day's fire you will ignite.

---

[251] reference to the title of Philip K. Dick, *Do Androids Dream of Electric Sheep?*

[252] "With electrons and positrons (or "holes") being created out of literally nothing, just ripped out of the quantum vacuum by electric fields themselves,..." —a restatement of Lawrence Krauss

[253] sexiness, sweetness, colours—don't exist:

[254] "(forward) Time travel is easy, just go to sleep." —Leonard Susskind

Be still and listen.[255] In the upper rush of fractals[256] and Mandelbrot sets[257]
my ionic[258] synapse chains pray :

> Designer-less chance, oh intelligence-less and purposeless void
> "I beg of you."
> Pray give me the hap and its ablauted hope to go forth and carry through,
> With the brain's soul moulded by monkey algorithms, to carry on.
> Oh self-reference I pray to You
> And make the Sun go through to the morrow.

> What will happen after that, will it mean 'the end of the universe'? (paraphrased) "'Nothing as trivial as that,' said the old man, calmly." —*The Hitchhiker's Guide to the Galaxy*

Poem 96   *2014/03/25.*

Even the Fowl Are Evil

> "Scientists have done experiments with rats in a cage and the floor of the cage was a hot-plate. These scientists would increase the heat on the hot-plate and invariably the rats would attack the weakest rat in the cage. They repeated the experiment in different countries and got the same result." —whitepaper

...It's not just man,

Even the little birdies are evil.

And how does retarded Abrahamic religion explain that off? Yes, even the little birds in the trees are evil. I know so. Because I "found out."

Flashback to bird-trap :

Bird comes for food taking and is trapped in wire-cage.

Hot sun burning down. Three little birds trapped. Blackbird, Bluejay, Starling.

Summer burning, birds panting, seeing me in terror. Blackbird and Bluejay go jumping about, fluttering crazy. Starling is quiet and keeps over in the corner.

I pick up cage. And try to shake them dead.

They watch me. Beaten up.

Then, what do they do? Blackbird walks over and picks on and pecks on Starling in the head. Bluejay follows next.

Starling was the passive and peaceful one. He fights back not. Off to the side. Hoping they will lay off.

I shake up box again. And then the banged-up birds walk over and stab Starling again.

Then I shake up box more. And sit it down, again.

Then Starling gets picked on to death. As I hover over and they fear.

I leave the two victors behind to bake to death in the burning summer Sun.

...And you are those birdies and I am those birdies. Those birds are me. I am in them and they are in me. As much as my blood is warm red and I am mammal.

Poem 97   *2014/04/08.*

The *Nomos* and the *Chronos* and the *Nómisma*, of the *Kósmos*

---

[255] Rumi (fyi: *rumi* means Roman.)
[256] fractals repeat.
[257] A Mandelbrot set is a recursive rule.
[258] ifc.unam.mx/Brain/ionchan.htm. Greek *Ion* means "to go". An ion is an extra electron attached to an atom. AKA, a thought.

"You are—your life, and nothing else." —Sartre, *No Exit*

"Tell me something. Knowing what you know. *How do you live with it?*"
"I try to focus on survival."

"The name of the" world, is *you*. You are the world.
You are the only world there will ever be by.
Forget the news events and governments. It doesn't matter.
And your world is going by, only, now. —The ablaut of new.[259]
Your hair will be white by the time the Other world's news comes to fruition.

And, the time of the world—the space of the world—the time of the world, is now. —Whose decision-tree[260] nodes branch out in binaries. Binary info bits[261] of yes OR no's (Claude Shannon's 1 or 0). Branching[262] out, the limitless tree.
So get, at, binary yes-or-no's. To get, at, the first node[263] of now. And then, and only then,[264] the position, to get, at, the next, *new* node… "Formula of our happiness: a Yes, a No, a straight line, a goal…" (Nietzsche)

And, so, the currency in the spacetime of the name of the world (*mundo*) is information—new (*modo*) info. (Hegel taught that truth is currency that you bring out to pay your way.) The opposite of information is called noise.[265] All the news-media's noise, it's all "just noise."

> "Anytime you face a difficult problem, you can ask: 'Do the laws of physics say solving this problem is impossible?' If the answer is no, then you know that there's only one thing in between you and the solution: knowledge. And thanks to Karl Popper, we know the only way to create knowledge is through trial and error. Conjecture and refutation. Guess and check, and guess again."

> "It's all about the bucks, kid. The rest is conversation." —Gordon Gekko

Poem 98 *2014/04/09.*
Whereby, Being Unique
Be means by.[266] Being unique, being different, is "a double-edged sword." ("Cuts both ways.")
You get cut by the blade of being strange.
But
You can cut by the blade of being novel.
And, as in the sentence grammar shows,
Whereby the verb (action)
Is by which the governor (of the arguments).[267]

---

[259] an *ablaut*
[260] Hopefully of Cladistic parsimony, https://wikipedia.org/wiki/Maximum_parsimony_(phylogenetics).
[261] In science, "a bit is a yes or no question, up or down, plus or minus." —Leonard Susskind
[262] "compare pairs of symbols for equality or inequality, & 'branch' (behave conditionally on the outcome of such tests)" — "conditional logic"
[263] Histories move in punctuated leaps or "nodes". —Hegel
[264] "event driven"
[265] Term 'noise' in 'information theory', aka "random info". ...Definition of information: "Information is a difference that makes a difference." —G. Bateson
[266] etymology of *be* is the preposition *by*. & its ablaut.
[267] wikipedia.org/wiki/Government_(linguistics) "Verbs govern their objects, & more generally, heads govern their dependents."

Whereby is by which.[268] By which!

> "O day and night [both], but this is wondrous strange. And therefore as a stranger give it welcome." —*Hamlet*

Poem 99 *2014/05/01. North America.*

Sometimes a Great *Nostos*

In the galley of the jet

to be landing soon.

In the clouds looking down at the grids of homes

methinks the turn is complete.

Now home go it and homebody errands

to soothe up and recoup.

The grave of routine sites revisited and revised.

Finding out for me who landed now

and but also finding out for connectome me who was there before this now me.

> "We shall not cease from exploration / And the end of all our exploring / Will be
> to arrive where we started / And know the place for the first time." —T.S. Eliot

Poem 100 *2014/07/04. U.S.A.*

Thinking at 90 IQ's

> "Why do people read? The answer, as regards the great majority, is: 'They don't.' The majority of
> mankind read nothing at all; of the remainder, the majority read only the picture papers. Of those
> who read something more than picture papers, the majority never gets as far as books. All the
> readers of books … all put together are a very small fraction of the population." —Bertrand Russell

Thinking at 90 IQ's, I listen to the puffed up barking preacher, and resonate with it.

Thinking at 90 IQ's, I read some scriptured up jew-bible lines, and have gullible believery.[269]

Thinking at 90 IQ's.

Thinking at 90 IQ's, I am manipulated fooled and feared to vote for *economy* issues and jobs

and anti-tax-and-spend issues and Freedom issues or gay issues—while my identity group

and culture go extinct.

Thinking at 90 IQ's.

Thinking at 90 IQ's, I read books not, I am an air-head ; a zero—an empty set.

Thinking at 90 IQ's.

Thinking at 90 IQ's, the propaganda framing and Orwellian lingual domination and Agendas,

are

Invisible to me,

And—they—form my frames,

Thinking at 90 IQ's.

Thinking at 90 IQ's, I obey think the war was because of WMD, like the, Right-side said.

—Or because of oil/money, like the Left-side said to mind.

—Thinking at 90 IQ's.

Thinking at 90 IQ's, I am a "*goy*-head."

---

[268] *whereby* means *by which*.
[269] the *Scofield Bible* scam. [wikipedia.org/wiki/Religiosity_and_intelligence]

Like the zombified European young-men eating *halal* butchered *sharma* outside of countless "*kibab* shops".[270]
—Thinking, thinking, I'm
Thinking at 90 IQ's.
The dummy-man—the universalist.

> "In conversation with him, one virtually feels that one is dealing not at all with him as a person, but with slogans, catchwords, and the like that have taken possession of him. He is under a spell, blinded, misused, and abused in his very being. Having thus become a mindless tool, the stupid person will also be capable of any evil and at the same time incapable of seeing that it is evil." —Bonhoeffer

Poem 101   *2014/07/15. U.S.A.*

Lose Your Illusion

The day you lose your illusion,
Is the day you are disillusioned. —Accepting reality's doom.[271]
The opposite of illusion is disillusion. —A but, you are blinded by emotions.
So, you can't see the facts of the truth, going on all begirdling you your life long. —Can't see the relative comparative differences.
Differences—which is the very definition of information. —You are blind to them.
Your eyes are blind with bias towards your perceived self
And emotionality. So you be not,
Disillusioned.

Poem 102   *2014/07/16. U.S.A.*

Walking the Tomes

In the library, walking the tomes. Walking by them ; walking past them.
The long line of books, shelves ; all the books ; in neat order.
I see all the rows and rows of books in the library.
Some Pareto 80 percent are dumb story-books. Bad stories. That had no fame.
Even most of the sellers, are just dumb stories.
Rows and rows of big story-books.
As I walk by them all...always...methinks how all of these dumb story-books were written by that statistical social-construct[272] mix called that deracinated word "whites."
Almost all the authors, all the names, are whites, and "European Jews" (*Ashkenazim*), or whatever stripe of *blancos*.
Maybe not good books. But I walk by them in admiration. Admiration, and respect.
—All the storybooks—they were thinking and thinking and writing their little novel. In their little lives.
Countless books. So many lives. Mostly all Europidal.
So many "Black" *mulattoes*. For five hundreds of years in America. And now. And *indio* Mexicá. But almostly no books.

---

[270] https://lbc.co.uk/article/charlene-downes-missing-girl-blackpool-case-reopened-DWzbQL_2/

[271] *doom/deem* means judgement

[272] wikipedia.org/wiki/Social_constructionism

All the rows and rows of bad story-books by *blancos*. Their books man the library.
Long dead authors of it all.
And me sees how all the folks milling about the streets are that social-construct mix called non-whites, now.
All these writers of no books. And, walking, I see I desire not their word.

Poem 103 *2014/07/17. Nebraska*

Bright, Sky, Blue
Blue clouds in the sky : Bright, sky, blue.
And you, I see in the
Bright, sky, blue : I see your, outs thoughts thinking.
You thinking you—your feelings : Blind, self-serving, feelings.
Not the bright, sky, blue.
The bright sky is here
This day.
But you
Thinking to-morrow. That day called to-morrow and to-morrow's descendents.
And are blind to me.
Not here. Fore me.
Bright, sky, blue.
I'm what's here
With the bright blue sky.

Poem 104 *2014/08/01.*

When

> "...knowing he'd unwound his string of days on earth…" —*Beowulf*

There has to come a time when a man decides to end it. There has to come a time.
A man has to end it. At some point. He has to end it.
As he gets old age-ed. And he has serious health *problema* ; with no support *systema*.
He has to think about how to end it. Whilst he can.
It's called euthanasia.

Poem 105 *2014/08/21. USA.*

Looking at the Noughts
Looking through the nots. Seeing *them*.
Seeing all the is's that ended to nots.
An ex-girlfriend. A relationship that ended.
I'm still seeing her. And seeing the not. The things that could be, but are not.
The not is her. In my mind. Going on, doing the things she was.
Seeing her loveliness, doing her girly things.
Seeing the nots. And the other nots. Other beings.

Of is's that stopped being.[273]
But their not being goes on. Doing things.
I see them. I go on seeing them,
Seeing the nots,
Of never.

"Nothing nots." —Heidegger

The pain he felt in his chest was her being dying. —para. Orwell, 1984

Poem 106 *2014/09/09. Somewhere over Europa*
Chain of Feeling
The heart agonises, "I don't understand."
—The core cries, "I don't understand."
I don't understand, regret weeps, "Why?"
I don't understand, agonises, "Why?"
Why, weeps, "I hate."
Why, agonises, "I hate."
I hate, answers, "I won't care."

Poem 107 *2014/10/19.*
Fishing For
Throw out, out, out the net. In, in, into the space.
Open the net wide. And net something. Something here, something there, something then.
Your neural net. Open it wide.
Out out out, in in in.
The neural network, called self.

[In Japan, the pond goldfish are called koi. And, koi means love in Japanese… And in India
Buddhism, the fish is a symbol of the Self. Which rises slowly to the surface from deep below.]

Poem 108 *2014/10/29.*
Forget the History?
"The fall of Stalingrad was the end of Europe. After that you can say that
white civilization was finished, really washed up." —L. F. Céline

"Forget the history!," your ex-girlfriend said.
Forget the history? —But the history never ends.
It's what's killing you now. —Being on the wrong side of WWII.[274]
"Forget the history!," your ex-girlfriends say. —As they fuck their big-dicked / low-IQ,
high-T, African-Negroid boyfriends in Europe. —History's stigmergic Derridean "traces"[275]
in the present. And if the traces of the past are in the present, then the traces of the present
are in the future. —Doomed, indeed.

---

[273] For *Dasein*, potentiality for being is *is*. —Heidegger
[274] toqonline.com/archives/v6n4/FaussetteV6N47x10.pdf .
[275] wikipedia.org/wiki/Trace_(deconstruction) / newderrida.wordpress.com/2007/11/19/some-key-terms/

Forget the history? No. The history keeps going on. It never stops.

Poem 109 *2014/10/29.*

The Abrahamic 'God's Image'

All of the scripts, all of the scribes. Stories, poems.

"Man was created in God's image." (*b'tzelem Elohim* "in the image of God")

All of the love hymns, all of the religion.

All of the soul and all of the spiritual : "Man was created in God's image."

All through the (Abrahamic) ages, and all of the (Abrahamic) holymen : "Man was created in God's image."

And then, after all this. We find that, yes, "Man was created in God's image."

—And that image, was a chimp. That's god. —God : He's the most despicable, low, ugly, and wretched of animals.

Now we understand that vile *Torah*-bible of genocidalism,[276] and its authors.

> "The ape, vilest of beasts, how like to us!" —Ennius, pre *AD*

Poem 110 *2014/10/29.*

Hegel's Duel : Who, What, When, Where, Why, and hoW

When did my writing die? Means, *where* did my writing die?

It's always a where.[277] *Das Sein* (Heideggerian "being there") died when he went a wanting.

—That was wherefore. That was the place.

Whysoever? He wanted something, at that time. At that place.

How so?[278] So he gave over,

But I[279] lost. That's who so.

That was wherover my consciousness died, withered. Hegel's "master-slave duel" (*Herr-Knecht*).

Whatsoever? Consciousness—writing.

At that time (when)—whither that place (where).

> "What is here, dost thou know it? / What was, hast thou known?
> Prophet nor poet / Nor tripod nor throne
> Nor spirit nor flesh can make answer, but only thy mother alone.
> Mother, not maker, / Born, and not made; / Though her children forsake her,
>   …
> But this thing is God, / To be man with thy might,
> To grow straight in the strength of thy spirit, and live out thy life as the light.
> I am in thee to save thee, / As my soul in thee saith;
>   …
> O children of banishment, / Souls overcast,
>   …
> I that saw where ye trod / The dim paths of the night
> In your skies to give light; / But the morning of manhood is risen, and the shadowless soul is in sight.
> The tree many-rooted / That swells to the sky
>   …

---

[276] *Rassenkampf,* Ludwig Gumplowicz

[277] "Where" is always going on because your "hippocampal location". …also, *wh*-items are quantifiers

[278] "Therefore" started out as "therefor" and means something like "for this [reason]". "Thus" and "so" mean "in this manner". "Hence" means "from here".

[279] switching the deixis. wikipedia.org/wiki/Deixis

The life-tree am I; / In the buds of your lives is the sap of my leaves: ye shall live and not die." —"Hertha", Swinburne

Poem 111 *2014/11/01.*

Needing to Go 'Take a Shit'

Sometimes I need it.

I get the feeling that I want to.

You *know* the feeling.

The urge ; to unload.

It's only a biological thing.

And then I do it and get it over with, and done with.

I call up that girl, that girlfriend—that fuck-buddy,

And we meet and I dump my load.

Like the feeling like needing to go take a shit.

Nothing to be happy about. Quite sad.

Only a fuck-buddy. Nothing more.

Just shit. —And the feeling of needing to "take a shit." That's all.

—An "open relationship" they language it. With a girl that doesn't know anything and has nothing to say.

Poem 112 *2014/11/02.*

What's Out There?

I've been everywhere. All the countries. A'round the world.

All the cities I wondered about : The far away places and folks. That

Loomed so large in my mind. My imagination. My curiosity.

Getting lost inside more cities. —I've been everywhere a'round the world, everywhere.

Everywhere. ...Even the ugly australoid Timor island in the South Pacific.

And I have come back with the *answer*.

I can tell you what I discovered.

I will tell it to you :

There is nothing out there.

There's nothing out there. Nothing.

"*Caelum non animum mutant qui trans mare currunt.* (They change their sky, not their soul, who rush across the sea.)", writ Horace.

Poem 113 *2014/11/29.*

The Ledger

Femme love says "no" to its hate. Butch anger replies, "who groomed you to love your abuser?"

When the last stone grinds the gravel away into dust, anger will be there grinding.

When soupy love yields all its last value up off out away to the last worthless destroyers, anger will not miss it.

As anger feels the destruction and crimes that self-centred love submits to, anger will see it.

—Anger, and anger alone.

The Western world mad with love, fooled with love, goes down, and gives its ass.

While anger is told to hide. —Honest and alone, with the reality of it all.

Anger, only anger. —The register.

Poem 114 *2014/12/01. Polska.*

The Jester's Answer

The legendary jester, that self-same legendary holy fool, he went 'round.

The joker met the queens, and saw that they were queens. And queens they were!

And, funniest of all, the joker met the kings, and saw that they were kings. And kings they were!

And the joker traversed to-and-fro the fore-and-aft of the courts the whole kingdom 'round,

and saw all what were. The joker met them all and received all their judgments.

Then and, and then,

The joker laughed and said, "They're all a joke." And the joker answered back, in return, "I'm a joke." "It's all a big joke." And the joker laughed and wept. Alone.

...Then and the earth shook and the land split and the whole kingdom came falling down and was swallowed up and rolled up into a bright spinning scroll.[280]

"Only when men shall roll up the sky like a hide, will there be an end of misery; unless the self has first been known." (*Upanishads*)

> "Some learned men, deluded, speak of nature, and others of Time; but it is the greatness of the self-luminous, self-existent one by which this wheel of Brahman is made to turn." —*Upanishads*

Poem 115 *2014/12/20.*

No-brainland

No-brainland is such a big place, so many folks.

No-brainland is an awful place, it's essentially brainless.

There are so many no-brainers in no-brainland that it is overcrowded.

Does no-brainland need any more folks? No.

So "swear off" no-brainland.

Don't help them, don't feed them, don't propagate them.

"Cut them off" from the land of the living brainers.

And don't breed with them, don't make more of them.

It is better that ye be an evolutionary dead-end, than making more of no-brainland. That crass, barren, illiterate place.

Poem 116 *2014/12/22.*

With All Thy Getting

With all thy getting, there's got to be something with interesting somewhere.

Who's got the knowledge to gift with, somewheres.

It's got to be somewhere around the corner, down the next empty grey street, somewhere or to-morrow.

To be got at by the right way, or chance, or created even.

It might be got-with even hidden in some book to read, or within some codes of *lógos*,[281] even.

---

[280] *the world rolls up into a scroll* —wordings of *The Last Judgement*

[281] eurocanadian.ca/2014/12/axial-age-and-european-discovery-of-logos-part2.html —Duchesne

(*lógos*; from λέγω, *légō*, lit. "I say")

There's got to be an expression or experience or sight, somewhere.

There's got to be something with interesting, somewhere, from without or from within all the empty grey existence[282] of all thy getting.

Poem 117 *2014/12/23.* PR: <u>YouTube.com/watch?v=VUoXtddNPAM</u>

The House that Jack Bought

Buy into the American life.

Be an atomised individual and buy into the American life.

Live in a house and be an atomised individual and buy into the American life.

Drive in a car and live in a house and be an atomised individual and buy into the American life.

Eat food and drive in a car and live in a house and be an atomised individual and buy into the American life.

Shop in a store and eat food and drive in a car and live in a house and be an atomised individual and buy into the American life.

Work in a job and shop in a store and eat food and drive in a car and live in a house and be an atomised individual and buy into the American life.

Pile-up money and work in a job and shop in a store and eat food and drive in a car and live in a house and be an atomised individual and buy into the American life.

Be phoney[283] and pile-up money and work in a job and shop in a store and eat food and drive in a car and live in a house and be an atomised individual and buy into the American life.

> "...but - do the houses in themselves hold any guarantee that *dwelling* occurs in them?" —Heidegger

Poem 118 *2014/12/25.*

Sláva Dnipro

I sailed upon a passenger boat, up the river Dnipro ;

And off the boat I did step and strolled the park of mansion Yanukovych.

The parks the greens the ponds the scenes, the *sláva* ("glory"), were not for me to have.

But have them I had, and took them all in, and basked in the bright sunray ; gloried in the bright sunray :

"Out of SPACE—Out of TIME." (EA Poe) —A boat ticket-price for-a-song.

"Out of SPACE—Out of TIME." —A life snatched out from the doom-and-gloom of its U.S.A. nativity.

"Out of place"—"out of synch." —I the expatriate *Amerikanisch* European.

A life snatched out from the *multikulti* U.S.A. machine (*Machenschaft*, Heideggerian "machination").

Saved by *sláva*.[284] *Salv* by *sláva*. In the bright sunray.

Poem 119 *2014/12/30.*

When Andy Warhol Said 'So What' in Bali

---

[282] (*Dasein*)

[283] Heiddegger's "inauthentic". Baudrillard's *Simulacrum*: <u>w2.bcn.cat/bcnmetropolis/arxiu/en/paged9fa.html?id=21&ui=363</u>

[284] *Slava* means glory. & *Slav*, the name of the tribe.

All the *I*'s that were me are still in me—in memories. Memories of those *I*'s that are not me anymore. The bad memories, the blunders, the ignorances, the brainlessness that got used, the loser. All those *me*'s that are not me. They are still with me, as memories. Bad memories, losses, regrets, waste. The *I* that is now me cannot forget—kill—those previous *I*'s, even though they are not me now. The best off that the *I* that is me can do is say, "So what," to them. When something happens, it is I who judges it for good or for bad. I choose how to judge it. So rather than as bad, and harm myself, just say, "So what." "In Bali, when a person dies, they do not weep and wail. They throw a party and celebrate."

> "There is nothing either good or bad, but thinking makes it so." —Shakespeare

Poem 120 *2014/12/31.*

The Voice of Inanimate Matter

"Once upon a time" I came to think that I am just a programme. This programme "I am who am" recursive tautology is just a word machine. "What's the next cognitive token?"[285] The word machine uses words—which are functions/mini-programmes. These words/functions are also especially the predicates/verb-phrases. —Predicates using Predicate Logic to pass typed arguments[286] into the predicates/functions. These predicates, and other vocabulary words, instantiate objects from inherited classes (*via* categories[287] or relational keys?)[288] or even abstract classes[289]—universals—that is to say, concepts. How else do these functions operate to take new space? How else does logic work with space? By using the recursion[290] of language. —Using addendums *ad infinitum* to forge new territory. —The typist in our minds—a neural net of weighted "next token prediction." And unlike nouns, all predicates are inherently binary, create binaries. Or, so anyways, as to my "line of thinking," from the book-readings of the texts. All the while being truth-tested[291] by feedback from the environment,[292] be it Bayesian or backpropagation. And adding new information ; and refactoring[293] of the logic—the binary if-then's—with memories.

Poem 121 *2015/01/03. ulitsa Miodowa, Kraków*

Non Binaries : Inside 'the Excluded Middle' [294]

It is said in Physics that there are no contradictions in the universe. And in Logic, contradictions are false, because two particular objects cannot occupy the same particular space at the same time. But what about the case of *one* honey-jar in *one* spot?
There's a honey-jar on the table-top that's looking, half-empty and half-full.

---

[285] autoregressive (AR) next tokenisation
[286] a programming technique of passing arguments into functions. ….Programmer's brains don't use the "language network" part of the brain for writing code, even though code has some similarities to natural languages. MRI studies show a different part of the brain called the "multiple demand network" is active during coding. This network is involved in complex cognitive tasks like solving puzzles and seems to be more suited to handling the logic and structure of code.
[287] wikipedia.org/wiki/Prototype_theory
[288] Relational Database theory uses keys & foreign-keys.
[289] Object Oriented Programming theory
[290] linguistics recursion
[291] wikipedia.org/wiki/Criteria_of_truth
[292] wikipedia.org/wiki/*Umwelt*
[293] a programming technique of improving the logic
[294] wikipedia.org/wiki/False_dilemma   wikipedia.org/wiki/Law_of_excluded_middle

Or *mead*[295] as they call it in non-English continental *Europa*.

When did mead stop being called mead and "from the off"[296] being called honey (Norman Conquest French *via* Roman Empire conquest), and why? It feels like a loss.

The answer is, that it never stopped being called mead.

It was just lost out. When the new name(er), Kripki's "necessity of identity," started winning over.

Now to be found out again in a different land where it, they, never lost.

Not true. Not false. (No good. No bad.) But both—that is to say, it's relative (to the side).

—Is the answer to the Logician's riddle, "This sentence is false." [297]

And, "if you choose not to decide [a side], you still have made a choice." (Neal Peart)

Two rocks from heaven ; two rocks from hell.

—Two blocks away from heaven ; is two blocks nearer to hell.

If and only if there is an *if*, then there is a *then*. (cause and effect; antecedent and consequent)

Where there is a one, then there is an Other.

> "The fetter of the heart is broken, all doubts are dissolved, all his works (& their effects)
> perish when he has been beheld who is high and low (cause & effect)." —*Upanishads*

Poem 122 *2015/01/09.*

Heġemony, On You

Heġemony[298] cometh, before you were born, born into it.

Heġemony that tore you up and tore you apart.

Heġemony that destroyed you and all you were.

Now you are here, peering outside, the heġemony.

Privy to the flipside of, the heġemony.

Privy to its lies and machiavellian machinations ; of text, framing, logic, history, media, emotion, and all that can be apostrophised here.

Heġemony working on all around you, capitalising. (—Where the only values is, money —the "value-added principle" (is a dollar of value added, or not?).) [299]

Babbittry.

Get in line, feel, follow—the heġemony.

Brainwash, propaganda—heġemony of empty signifiers—is war "to the bone".

Warfare by words ; heġemony, total and complete.

Winners *versus* losers. —Which be you'uns?

I turn the wheel of Mind.

Poem 123 *2015/02/10. America.*

'It Must Have Been Hell'

---

[295] (Proto-Indo-European "wet")
[296] "From the off" evolved from the older, unstressed form of the word "of," which originally meant "away from".
[297] wikipedia.org/wiki/Liar_paradox
[298] Gramscian "Cultural Hegemony"
[299] Alain de Benoist

"There was a child went forth every day,"[300] in America they be called trailer-park trash. In Europea they be called "villagers". Hillbilly's. The low-class, the uneducated, the delinquent, the ignorant, …the poor. That was the function-pronoun *him*, as a child. —Trailer-trash. Totally deprived—of all. But told he had an "anger problem." No parents 'round. A throwaway kid sitting outside a gas-station at 12 at night, eating a candy-bar and sipping a cola—his supper. Always alone. Never given music lessons, or a book. —Never *told* of a book. Only U.S.A. circumcised after birth and taught early to worship the jew-Jesus and sent at 15 to go work in a sweat-shop. —That's about all. All the consciousness level of a dog. Growing up on candy and soda-pop and an antenna-TV in an empty room with nobody home. In a trailer-park trash existence. —That was him, *in toto*. Reading the back of a box of cereal at 2 in the morning. Nobody ever sent *him* to Summer-camp.

Poem 124 *2015/01/25.*
The Bowels of Shame

> "A great proportion of the misery that wanders in hideous forms around the world, is allowed to rise from the negligence of parents; " —*Frankenstein*

Through the bowels of shame, comes forth the new man.
Through the rancour-stench of his past, swirling the drain, rises memories of the future.[301]
As the man gropes forward and falls and crawls the pathless curse of his misbegotten parentage, which is destiny, caste in *stein*.
Movement through the bowels of shame, comes forth the feelings,
Which beget, his awareness and appraisals, towards his new appraisals and re-alignments and direction.
Leaving his errant scat path behind him.
More and more moving now on a path of his own making and form.
Feeling the bowels of shame, is this life-long, passing—through—the wasteland, of his soiled origines—parentage.
And, when he dies, all those memories of moments will be lost in time, like turds flushed down the toilet.

Poem 125 *2015/02/05.*
Falling into Slots

Walking and walking.
Falling into place—go my steps of my feet.
Slots of walking and slots of steps and slots of words and slots of thoughts and slots of electrons.
The slots, are mine, to fall into, all mine.
Thinking, in sentential, the word tagmemes,[302] are mine, to fall into, the slots, of the syntactic

---

[300] Walt Whitman
[301] Plato: the truth is *remembered*
[302] tagmeme: a type of grammatical analysis based on the concept of function in sentence **slots** & the determination of classes of words that can fill each **slot**. well-formedness: wikipedia.org/wiki/Grammaticality

grammar[303];
Fall, fall, following … the laws.
Like how electrons go falling into electron-holes.[304]
The words upon the law syntactics rest—floaters bobbing on the stream of consciousness.

Nietzsche wrote, "I am afraid we are not rid of God because we still have faith in grammar."
—We believe in god because we believe in grammar—subject-verb. God is the ultimate subject.

This thing we are using—word's grammar—it is our whole lives. How we could live without knowing about it? Like what "a" means and does in a sentence. —An indexical position, a preposition, meaning one instance. Or concatenating "a" as a one to mount on an "unmarked" word so it becomes opposite positioned/meaning. —The "primate mounting behaviour" of human logic. *A* is a particle, marking particularism off from general universalism, an instantiation from the non-existent.

> "We have used words all our lives in certain patterns, and instead of calling the patterns 'rules', we attribute the courses of our thought processes to the 'meanings' of words." —Hofstadter, *Godel, Escher, Bach*

> "The law is to obey the will of the One [Zeus]." —Heraclitus

Poem 126 *2015/02/15.*
Reality Tracking
At *café*. Helping a woman on with her coat—it's an affectation—it's performative—it's transactional. It's not real—it's not power.
I don't help a woman on with her coat. I'm not an actor.
I'm not an actor—I'm in-search of the real.
I'm in-search of the *meta*-real that's underneath all the affectations.
That's the know-how I'm into fetching.
Fetch your own coat.[305] I'm here now for the real of *my time* for me.
Not like a weak man who must play board-games or cards or picnic or action-rides with another person because he's too empty-headed and unreal to engage in interesting talking.
See the energy in my eye.

Poem 127 *2015/02/16.*
All the That's Not There
What's a that's not there?
There's a that's not there. And there's another that's not there.
There's some that's not there wherever you look.
Whatever you see ; there's that's not there all around.
All the things you see are there, and material and concrete.
But lots of their *qualia* you see, like colours, are not there. (Goethe's "Theory of Colours" was

---

[303] wikipedia.org/wiki/Agreement_(linguistics)
[304] electron holes: wikipedia.org/wiki/Charge_carrier
[305] wikipedia.org/wiki/Imperative_mood

wrong.) Just like sounds are not there. —Only your brain creates them.[306]

And numbers are not there ; and the words in your head talking to yourself, thoughts, are not there.

Concepts and categories and patterns, are not there.

And especially you—your self, the analogue-I and the analogue-me—is

Not there.

Poem 128 *2015/02/16.*

Crooking My Eyebrow

Small shot-glasses roll sideways as they fall.

Ascue people meet and mix and match, and match not, and part ways.

Not for a "coffee, *chai* [!]" they *café*. (The street-stall chant in Russkiy-speaking Eurasia.)

They *café* to match or split or crook or and.

Game theoretic, "Here today, gone tomorrow." "Take a shot" "and see" ;

The small shot-glasses rolling sideways as they fall.

Poem 129 *2015/02/21.*

Pro [307]

> "For when I speak, I introduce opposition. ...Reality I cannot express in speech, for
> to indicate it I use Ideality, which is a contradiction, an untruth…" —Kierkegaard

To meet someone is to meet their agenda. To interface

With someone is to interface with their agenda. To talk

With someone is to talk to their agenda. To hark

What they say and think

Is to be manipulated

Towards their frame

Fore their agenda.

Spurious things, obedience and submission.

Morals go relative to the subjection.[308]

The text moves forward as the mind follows. As we fall under its spell.

Or a man's voice stands up using the language at its command

and we stand-under its point-of-view stance.

Spurious things is morality.

It is only what works ; and what's good for you'uns.

"I" is a self-reference to an I.[309]

"Me" is a recursion to some me.

"We" is a circular reasoning to some we.

---

[306] Colours & sounds are created by the human mind. —This is undisputed in the scientific community.

[307] "for"/fore. ...See "motivated reasoning"

[308] The grammatical structure of this sentence: go_relative(morals, to the subjection) —One predicate, the verb phrase, is like a programmer's function with 2 arguments.

[309] *I* is a "personal pronoun".

"Our" is a tautology to the our.

"You" is recursion to which you? Are you the you in the you of you?

In linguistics all pronouns are recursive.[310]

And what does that say of "you" and "your" truths?

Even when an author is masking himself in some social construct or some concept or some Other character's proper names.[311]

—Self-referentiality being contradictory.[312]

Poem 130 *2015/02/22.*

What's in the Past is Perfect

A part of the *praxis*—an interconnection—that's now past-perfect.

"Collapsing the wave functions," as they say.

—When eyes flashed light and eyes met and coffee was drunk as the two marginal utility maximising agents talked a connection, then the parting.

But "always already"[313] a part of the *praxis* of the past-perfect tense, for-ever.

The past-perfect tense is forever and ever, perfectly.[314]

Poem 131 *2015/02/23.*

Universal *versus* Particular

It's a universal fact that everything is particular. Hear me now :

In the debate betwixt universalist *versus* particularist, only the particular matters :

Sometimes the real (the physical world) is true ;
Sometimes the real is not true.

Sometimes the true is real ;
Sometimes the true is not real.

But in the real (the physical world), only the true real counts.
Just as in the true, only the real (physical) true counts.

They are always the same, but, in both, only the particular matters.

["For 'true' and 'false' are attributes of speech, not of things. And where speech is not, there is neither 'truth' nor 'falsehood': 'error' there may be," —Hobbes, *Leviathan*

"Locke makes a distinction of truth into *real* and *verbal*: meaning by the former the agreement of things as they exist in nature, and by the latter the agreement between our conclusions and the language in which they are uttered."]

Poem 132 *2015/02/24.*

The Illiterati

---

[310] wikipedia.org/wiki/Anaphora_(linguistics) pronouns are anaphoric

[311] proper nouns/names: Causal theory of reference —The "Historical Chain Theory" (Best for referent to person, place, thing.)

[312] wikipedia.org/wiki/Principle_of_explosion

[313] wikipedia.org/wiki/Always_already

[314] wikipedia.org/wiki/Perfect_(grammar)   wikipedia.org/wiki/Grammatical_tense

If you could hark the musing *musica*, you could cite it.
Like gay Walt Whitman did, so verbosely.
But you don't (cite it) because you can't (hark it).
You can't harken or see or cite, or even read it.
So we people on, *en masse*. Crass and evil and short-sighted and cheating and projecting.
But clutter outside us ; and (because), but clatter inside us.

Poem 133 *2015/02/25.*
Murky has Woken

> *I. Rise and Shine*

The murky water flowing sky, leads to another day.
My swimming thoughts of defections,[315] cycling.
Waking up—the animacy[316] of words ordering themselves into hierarchic (syntactic) sententials.
As the monkey me rise-and-shines to forage a new day.

> *II. Waking Up*

I woke in the morning.
  —The morning to my aching body and head.
I rose to my feet.
  —To kill the death in my bones and tiredness.
And forced *on* my mind.
  —The mind that brings into focus it's tasks for the day.
And rushed to the coffee-pot.
  —To rush finish a hot cup of strong coffee heavily milked and sugared.
A drink to quench my parched throat.
  —And jolt my throat and mind *on* from the *off* of dead.

> *III. Hyme at Sunrise*
>   "He who is the person in the sun, I am he [Brahman]." —*Upanishads*

In the vision of the Sun,
East, in the morning,
in the vision of the Sun,
in the vision of the Sun, is the many,
in the vision of the Sun,
the Sun, in the vision of the Sun,
the Sun, in the vision of the *Sonnen*,
the One,
the, Sun *esti* a vision of the One.[317]

---

[315] Game Theory
[316] wikipedia.org/wiki/Animacy
[317] YouTube.com/watch?v=g4Mzujd6aBw

The sun and the moon and the rain, she sings to me.
The sun, and the moon, and the rain, she sings to me-e-e.
The sky and the grass, she lives to be with me.
My mother, my earth, she lives for me-e-e.
Weather or not, yeah, I am not alone, as long, as I live, with her-r-r.
The sun, and the moon, and the rain, she sings to me-e-e.

Poem 134 *2015/02/26.*

Fear is Selfishness

Smile.

It's fear that says, "Hello." And it's fear that says, "Hello," but says not too much more as to "pay a cost."
It's fear that pays taxes,
And it's fear that does nice.
It's fear that goes to jobs ; fear of getting cancer.
It's fear of being alone, that makes for relationships.
And fear of getting old that makes us exercise.
It's fear that pays the *café* tips. And it's fear of being judged immoral (low) that makes us Politically Correct to losses of our identity interests.

> "Agreeableness is fear. Agreeableness is to reduce friction." —Curt Doolittle

Poem 135 *2015/02/28.*

Recalling[318] Yourself Talking to Yourself

> "A linguistic sign is not a link between a thing and a name, but
> between a concept and a sound-pattern." —de Saussure

Sounds are the memories of the sights of rocks thrown into ponds ; and all manner of such memories of sights are sounds. [all words are analogies (to a sounds)]
Sights . . . to word sounds (phonemes).
Nothing yawns that has not an identity, a proper name, a noun, or a pronoun to do it. (Kripke's "necessity of identity.")[319]
Can't there be anything, sentential, that has not a name, a noun?[320] (No.)
Verbs can't (imply) verb.
Only nouns can verb. Sentential-ly, verbally. (*lógos*; from *légō*, lit. "I say")
But verbs can (imply) noun.
And only objects can (imply) subject-noun and verb. —Meaning all objects need (come from) such. Are instantiated by such. In sentenceal grammar.
The judge says, "Carry out the sentence." —And stretched to the hardness of a noose—blindfolded, goes a "you" or an "I"—who are made subject.

· · · · ·

---

[318] The "law of calling" defines that "to **recall** is to call." (Spencer-Brown)
[319] 'An object (subject). A concept (predicate/function). …All sentences have a noun phrase & a verb phase.'
[320] 'An object (subject). A concept (predicate/function). *Alice is happy.* All sentences have a noun phrase & a verb phase.'

I dreamt I wrote a message in Frito chips. The short Fritos were the short words and the long Fritos were the long words.

Bit by bit ; I wrote the message all out in Frito chips.

All the Fritos were horizontal in perfect order and sizes ; line by line.

The pattern was in perfect order, but then I forgot—couldn't recall—the sound that each Frito stood for.

Poem 136 *2015/02/28.*

In Praise of Alleles

Thank-ZOG. I have the alleles not to be a Christian (*moshiach* worship) ;

To be able to see through the sham, easily.

The alleles to be able to see that I evolved to know (*gnosis*) the spiritual and to experience the spiritual, and do see (thus not a-gnostic) and do experience, even though they don't really exist, like *qualia* colours don't exist ; plus see this sham of bible texts operating on top of this neuro module ; thank-god.[321]

I would rather not live (or beget), if it meant a life-form inside of believing in that Abrahamic-serving religion's illusion. Even if that illusion afforded happinesses and payoffs. Thank-god for my alleles.

> "Yes, we have a soul. But it's made of lots of tiny robots." —Giulio Gioreli

Poem 137 *2015/03/20.*

The Facts of Existence

And the plant was planted and the plant grew and the Sun shone (on the plant and enriched the plant) and the plant said, "Sun, you exist."

And the Earth nourished the young plant and the plant said, "Earth, you exist."

And the village invested in the plant's growth and the plant said, "Village, you exist."

And the plant became a tree. And the tree matured into a big old tree, of strong wood and broad branches.

Then the ol' planter came 'round, with a li'l bucket o' water, to stand in the comfort of the old tree's shade.

And the shade-tree said, "No, you don't exist. ...I am old now and my growth complete, and have deep roots of my own. ...*There's nothing you can do for me now* (to-morrow was yester-day)... You should have watered the plant when it was younger, when it would have mattered materially, made a difference. You meant nothing to me. No, you don't exist to me."

And, *in fact*, that planter did *not* exist. Not to *that* tree.

> "Only let into your life the people who are helping your life." (C. Manson)

Poem 138 *2015/05/15.*

Just an Empty Chair

I think it's the emptiness in the faces that's the most painful thing to see.

---

[321] "metamagical thinking"

Empty faces of empty people ; a chock-full city of 'em ; filling the streets and buildings ; in all its grey-ety.

Seeing the Bulgakov "dog's heart" in the empty faces : faces combating to get their take ; winnings for nothings ; striving, "unto the bitter end."

Me too ; I look into the looking-glass ; and it ails me ; the vacuuity.

Event, to your best-friends, to them

You are

Just an empty chair.

Poem 139   *2015/09/09.*

A Grim Message from the Future

Whate'er betide, elders never say it, but, hearken, kid, I'm many years older than you, so, *I know*, because, I'm from the *futura*. I am talking to you from the future.

—I am older than you—so I am from the future, relative to you—talking to you from the future—I am in the future—because I am older and you are younger. —Like gay Walt Whitman addressing the reader from the Brooklyn ferry dock, "And you that shall cross from shore to shore years hence."

I tell you,

Every year it gets more and more black, more depressing, more and more dog-like ;

Every year, you know people are a little bit more corrupt and criminal and evil-selfish (transactional) than the year before ;

And you also know more that, as a human, you are evil. —"People are animals."

Like unto Wordsworth's "Intimations of Immortality", idealisms, romanticisms of youth become a forgotten memory.

It's depressing.

More and more, every year, a little more black.

Until you don't even check out your uglifying image in a mere looking-glass anymore. To look at that dog. The animal. And it's distorted point of viewing.

Kid, I know, because I'm from the future—to you—because I'm a lot more years older than you. For, "... you ... shall cross from shore to shore years hence."

> "Montaigne, said that ageing diminishes us each day in a way that, when death
> finally arrives, it takes away only a quarter or half the man." —Levi-Strauss

Poem 140   *2015/10/10.*

Zero on My Mind

Wasn't it Paul de Man who said that the definition of "zero", (which is $1/\infty$), "is the capacity for everything"? —Akin to Derrida's "blank piece of paper."

...I've "burned out." I've given up the hope for *the one* thing.

So I make no schedules and plans. So I anticipate nothing.

Because : I want to make sure that I wake-up every morning to

Zero. Sweet zero.[322]

---

[322] an empty placeholder, a name that allows everything to fold into it

Not zero the de Saussure's "sign"—the symbol—the referent. But to zero the de Saussure's "signified"—the thing, the experience. —Alain Badiou's "event."

That big blank *blanco* zero of the experient. That space for ("presencing") anything and everything.

Poem 141 *2015/11/10.*

A Critique of Pure Profanity

That old dichroic discourse, of, *the sacred and the profane*.

It's the "always already" binary (that we are at) of the creative vantage point *versus* the mundane vantage point :

The broad-minded perspective and the petty perspective : the artistic and the practical.

One view is hard to see and one view is easy to see.

It's all about the point of viewing.

(The practical, the practical, always thinking, focused, on the practical.

The practical is full[323] important, it is true ; but nearsighted.)

We are always fixated on the practical, but are blinded to the artistic (sacred spirit) view of life.

—That there is something more than just the petty practical focus and locus (of control).

The role of Arts in history

Has ever been to show us that there is something more than only just the practical.

If only practical, then we are just (controlled) dogs. No different in our position.

Poem 142 *2015/12/25. Europe.*

'It's All a Blur'

Racing flying time. Winding down. The big entropy.

The chromosomal clock ; peeling away its finite telomeres[324] of replications.

Stop in the street and try and think and see—is like looking out of a racing train's window-pane.

We can blurrily think and see what's going on out there and with ourselves that's never there but always moving along

Down the tracks. Towards destination death.

Poem 143 *2016/04/04.*

'The Devil's Dam[e]' [325]

Dame deceit came at me one day, on the telephone, in all of her Humanity.

And said with real feeling, "You need to know that forgiveness is the greatest thing in life! Forgiveness is such a wonderful thing to do. It helps you in so many great ways. All you need to do is just forgive. You need to just forgive (up *to* me)."

—And, quick, countered up my personal-pronoun *I* to dame deceit, "Ah, well, I see, ah-huh ah-huh. Will you forgive me for all of the terrible bad things that I have done to you?"

Dame deceit (was) halted and fell silent. And gave no answer. She gave not.

---

[323] *full* was the English word for *very*, before the French *very* started to be used.

[324] livescience.com/18613-cell-doomsday-clocks-cancer-nigms.html

[325] "...the devil's dam.." (Shakespeare) The devil's mother, was considered to be even more evil than the devil himself.

And, so outed, took me nevermore.

Poem 144   *2016/04/14.*
Parabolic Projection
Hot sense on cold water blows warm rain.
Yeah, Winter space is unpacking into Spring. (When Spring's thunder kills off Winter.
—"Spring kills Winter, usually with his sprinkler or his striker")
The *Jul* wheel, "the year comes rolling." (*Vedanta*)
Thoughts crystal, then clear away.
"Where did my time go or what does where mean?" The wetware machine says as it's
"embedded Aspect" reads it's output.

Poem 145   *2016/04/15.*
Esse Word : A Hypostasis Hypothesis
Is, "is what it is," or isn't it?
Is asks, "Is the '*a*' a 'the'?"
"And what or who or where or how is '*is*'?"
Is is *by*, we know. Like *I* be *me*.
And *the*-from-*a* from *is* does form. The particular *the* from the universal *a*. [indefinite article
('*a*'). definite article ('*the*').]
...As all words are variations of one word, the set of all sets is a set of itself ("Russell's paradox,"
of Frege). Or, as Leibniz said, "From one unity number all numbers are created."

> "As all leaves are attached to a stalk, so is all speech attached to
> the *om* (Brahman). *Om* is all this, yea, *om* is all this." —*Upanishads*

> "The name, once introduced, becomes the Mother of the Ten Thousand Things" —*Tao Te Ching*

Poem 146   *2016/04/21.*
Seeing a Fish in a Fishbowl
I see a fish in the water, three levels deep :

Fish of life—a glimmer in a speckle of water.
Life of fish—swimming in space in circles.

Fish eye—you have your place before you atomise away.
Eye sees fish eye sees—and swims its circle hungrily.

I see fish but I can't see my seeing eye—and fishbowl fish don't know about me.
The trinary level, "'I am the seer, and the seen,' the brahmin sings."[326]

Poem 147   *2016/07/07.*
The Divine Twins : Looking into the Eye of a Youth
> "The bud disappears when the blossom breaks through, and we
> might say that the former is refuted by the latter;" —Hegel

---
[326] subject, object

I live in a world of sunsets and dawnings, dawning on the setting of the sun.

Eye see the memories of what a clueless boy saw—in my "mind's eye."

—As he went clueless and helpless, a know-nothing, amongst the adults,

As the adults looked with feeling into his eyes and knew it.

—Knew their hopelessness and meanness, and knew the boy's—not knowing it now—destiny of being that too someday ; and so that boy, also knowing all that also (their meanness), someday.

—All this, as the adult would look with feeling at him, big-eyed, and pet his hair and say a nicety, and saw in themselves, their childhood, ageing, and old adulthood.

Eyeing a looking-glass reflecting into a looking-glass sees many countless looking-glasses, going back to no end. (As an infinite-series gets closer and closer to one.)

A world of sunsets and dawnings, dawning on the setting of the sun.

> The *Arya* horse riding "divine twins", originally Manu and Yemo—sunrise and sunset—the "sons of *Dyaús*"—pull the "solar chariot" of *Saulė* (Balt Sun) through the sky. ...One of the earliest engagements with the problem of the One and the Many is found in Parmenides metaphysical poem, "On Nature". The poem tells of a chariot drawn from night into day, from non-Being into Being.

Poem 148 *2017/08/22. Luxemburg.*

Sight-Seer : Anatomy of the Perfect Scenic-View

There sits *das Kirche-haus an der Strasse,*

A ragged beggar sunning ;

Sunset's yellow sclera[327] hitting its exact *nader*, glowing down-and-out.

Tonic clonic seized me midway long-torsoed "bridge Schlossbrücke," spying it. —From *erectus* cliff to *erectus* cliff, the alveolar arch struggles to bridge the prognathous jaw.

Horizon overlooking the broad deep valley with the recessive traited Uelzecht river *cours*[328] and filled to brim with old village mansions, shiny blue-black roofed. —Imagist, "Petals on a wet, black bough." (Ezra Pound)

Is at its greenest of the August. All the perfect peak of a scenic-view...

Suddenly : "Miguel Ugabugo should be three times that!"

—Twain British men marching up the long mediaeval brachycephalic-stone bridge to the ancient, Bock, bergtop city of Luxemburg. One imposing tall nordid blonde-type middle-aged barked to his counterpart short stocky dinaric-type Brit. Pass me by in a flash. Engaged in brisk back-and-forth chat on their march. And what are they talking about?

"Miguel Ugabugo should be three times that!"

—Not about culture, history, science, philosophy, literature, politics, life, people. No. Football. I, the seer, spy them at the same time as the great scenic-view, both at once. This *doppelgänger* scenic-view.

Standing I rotate away my head back to the peak scenic-view. Then I rotate 'round again.

I saw the face which shook me, and suddenly it was swart as dusk ; a moon-faced australoidal

---

[327] Only non-human apes and sufficiently full-blooded Sub-Saharan Africans have a yellow sclera.
[328] race

Indian stood before me and treaded past me, sneaking busy peeks at phone. Woman, "ugly as sin."

This giant Gothic stone bridge. In ruins. The seer looks all 'round now ; a "*europa* [all-seeing] *Zeus pater.*" [329] Still standing still.

The *gängers* multiply. More *colonos* ; more *le Grand Replacement*.

All in that *uno momento* of

The perfect scenic-view.

"As down dark tides the glory slides," —Tennyson

Poem 149 *2018/01/01. Luxemburg.*

Happy Father's Day

As your son barfs into the *vomitorium* of his memories, he remembers you.

You know (what), he loves not knowing you.

He really did hate you. Really, he wished you were dead. A long time already. (Decades and decades and decades.)

But he finally found (out) a way to love. He, "fuck-you money," nixed you (out) from his world,

And loves not knowing you. He loves not knowing you—that delinquency.

"Revenge is sweet." Justice "counts for something." He loves it. It's something to hold on to and to cherish. (Now he likes how you live a long, long time.)

The years roll bye. So happy not to know you.

As they say in English, "Now who's laughing?"

Your low-regard for him was because of your low-regard for so much of yourself you saw in him. (*para.* Jordan Peterson)

Money-talks, "I open my empty pocket, turn it inside-out, and find no forgiveness to give fore you."

"But above all he must refrain from seizing the property of others, because a man is
quicker to forget the death of his father than the loss of his patrimony." —Machiavelli

Poem 150 *2018/05/01. Waldbillig, Luxemburg.*

***Scène Desideratum* : As Seen from Outside the Afrofied Villages of Luxemburg**

I saw me a man jogging. In the sunny morning, the sight is surreally clear.

The sunny warm morn at the hilltop road-crossing, is photographic in my memory.

The bus-stop corner. A tiny Afrofied village each, opens at the ends.

In this countryside green, I saw me a man jogging.

The middle-aged stereotypical whiteman distance-runner in Spandex tights. He darts left (my right) from the edge of his path and picked up a plastic bottle.

To put in his other hand with another litter scrap.

Then, without slowing his fast pace, suddenly darted over to the trash-can by my bus-bench, and dumped them in. As he continued running down the country-road and off over the horizon, scanning for more litter.

---

[329] Daughter of Zeus, Goddess *Europa* means wide-eyed. Common phrase, "*europa Zeus pater*"

You see, he is wanting and wishing. A'wanting and a'wishing, to have a community. Wanting to have a society, a *familia*. Wanting to have a country. And wishing to help a'it and to make it better.

He simply couldn't help himself—he can't stop it. So he thinks he can one-man white-knight it into existence.

But he can't. His country's not like him now. He's a minority now. An altruistic outlier.

He is an European minority in a formally European homeland in Europe.

No *Solidarność* now. None. And never will again.

I saw me that jogger. Sad and pitiful—he simply couldn't stop himself. —He wanted . . . *he knew not what.*

...And reality being so isomorphic, a chain of interconnections, entanglements, next to this lonely bus-stop scene, is a U.S.A. flag, a big rock, a bronze plate, text. —Celebrating "American Victory", *"emancipation"*. *Rundstedt's Ardennes offensive (Battle of the Bulge), Wanter 1944/45.* "Wehrmacht." "The commune suffered heavily under the Nazi terror." "We honor[330] their memory."

But the *real* logic reads, the form[331] of the real scene, because reality is so isomorphic : *To the Americanising victors, to the fools who died in war fighting for the Africans who would Grand Replacement them.*

Poem 151 *2019/12/17. Kyiv.* YouTube.com/watch?v=iGw2gRfM1go

The Cuckolds : *'Arbeit Macht Frei'* from Seekers of 'Proximity to Whiteness' [332]
A German can only lie if he believes it is true. —para. Mark Twain

"Picture Africans as Turks. If *all* the Turks[333] in Turkey lived in Germany and *all* the Germans in Germany lived in Turkey, then all the Turks in Germany would want to go live in Turkey." And the blanking German blinks and does not understand and his mind goes back to work.

And again I sally, "If every particular German would go to a little island in the South Pacific *and* everyone in Germany was African, then *no* Africans in Africa would want to go to Germany ; and all the Africans in Germany would want to go to that particular little island in the South Pacific." (Seekers of "proximity to whiteness" as academia calls it.)

I say to the German, "They will follow you wherever you go!"

And the blanking German blinks and does not understand, but does not question.

So to-top-it-off, I quest for the German, "Do you know why?"

And the Last Man of Nietzsche's Zarathustra "blinks" a blank stare.

And through true-blue eyes[334] gazes earnestly, "channelling his inner *man of the Left*,"[335] and replies softly, "I don't know why."

---

[330] *Honor* printed in the USA spelling. Not the European English way, *honour*.

[331] wikipedia.org/wiki/Correspondence_theory_of_truth

[332] The pre-WWII Teutonic-speaking Europe *motto*. (*Mañana, mañana*, Latin-speaking-world *motto*.) Taken from the middle ages *motto* "city air makes free"; meaning a serf is declared legally free if he can live inside of a city for *1* year and *1* day.

[333] In Deutschland and Netherlands, "Deutsche-Turks" vote hard *Left* (liberal) in Germany. and, because they also can vote in Turkey, these same people vote, in large majority, hard *Right* (nationalist) in Turkey.

[334] Dutch expression "too blue-eyed" means gullible/*naive*, as well as in all the Teutonic languages, "*blauäugig*". ... Mediaeval folk assigned the colour blue with values loyalty and innocence.

[335] a line from "the prophetic" Houellebecq's *Submission*

And I say bluntly to the *blondinko* German, "It is because you are '..., the white race of 'Liberals' of every age...' (Nietzsche) ; you will never go free, they will follow you wherever you go!"

Befuddled, but Kantian (universalistically moral) *über alles* else, the *Gutmensch*[336] German blinks and his mindset blanks back to working on his tasks.

> "What makes Europe desirable to Africans is that they are not there. As they make landfall there *en masse*, it is no longer of interest to anyone: destroyed for Europeans, destroyed for Africans, it is a book that erases itself when opened." —Renaud Camus

More africans here

Than Europeans here

Poem 152 *2020/12/25. Kraków*

'Cause Locke[337] Rationalised the Jew of Tarsus's Christianity into Liberalism

Zion is watching.

OBEY Zion.

Zion is chosen (French *elite* cognates from *elect*, chosen).

"Our God is Your God Too, But He Has Chosen Us."

Kneel to Zion (Hebrew *zion* means "highest point").

Those who bless Zion will be blessed, those who curse Zion will be cursed (according to "the sacred scrolls").[338]

Take-a-knee to Zion.

Zion is watching you.

Zion shall close down your media accounts and financial accounts. ("Stakeholder" capitalism.)

Opposition to Zion is violence. Questioning Zion is hate.

Fear of Zion is the root of all wisdom.

Eye on Zion, the Zion king.

Zion will close down your communication accounts and financial accounts ; OBEY the ruling-class.

Zion is what Heidegger called "Machination."   The game theoretic phenomena of Mosca's "the circulation of the elites theory"[339] and Robert Michels' "iron law of oligarchy."

Poem 153 *2021/10/02. Kraków*

---

[336] wiktionary.org/wiki/*Gutmensch*

[337] "the father of Liberalism" —a Christian fanatic who put all Christian concepts into secular terms. John Locke taught that atheism should be completely illegal.

[338] An expression from the *1960*'s movie *Planet of the Apes*

[339] The replacement of one group's elites by another group's elites.

'Be Thou Our Offscouring' [340]

> "Some of them understand why, and some do not, but they all understand that their happiness, the beauty of their city, the tenderness of their friendships, the health of their children, the wisdom of their scholars, the skill of their makers, even the abundance of their harvest and the kindly weathers of their skies, depend wholly on this child's abominable misery." —Ursula LeGuin, "The Ones Who Walk Away From Omelas"

Outside the soup-kitchen, I mooted to the hobo *gringo blanco* sitting on the curb in the gutter, the ten-thousand dollar bill lying on the sidewalk that no one picked up, "Hey *amigo*, all these *enemigo mestizos* swarming in, they are taking over and pushing you out. You should organise and start an action to put an end to *la inmigración*. You should start something."
"No."
"Why not?"
"Fuck 'em (*los blancos*)."
"But soon they (*los indio mestizos*) are taking over if you don't do something. Why not?"
The hobo angrily out spake, "I'm not going to be their (*los blancos'*) Jesus so they can crucify me to die for their sins."
And the hobo caught "the light of consciousness" of the Holy One flash out from my face. Locking me in the egoless gaze, spoken that hobo, that selfsame homeless hobo, "My problem was that I cared. I cared too much. Nobody else cared. Nobody cared. I was the only one who cared. I shouldn't have cared."
And the hobo caught an empathy emote out off my face.
Found guilty, later I left home and walked away from Omelas, going nowhere.

> A Homeric epithet of Zeus (from *Deus* meaning light) is εὐρύοπα (*eurúopa*), meaning "wide vision". (In current English jargon, "the light of consciousness".) This epithet is the etymology of Europe itself, through Εὐρώπη (*Európē*) — a woman abducted by Zeus. The *Ṛg-Veda* presents *Dyáuṣ* (meaning light) as the "all-knowing god" as well. Thus, equipped with this power, the *Ṛg-Veda* acknowledges the greatness of the sky-god, whom is referred as *máh*, "great". A similar Homeric epithet, μέγας (*mégas*), is often applied to Zeus.

Poem 154   *2022/03/01. Kraków*

Not Everyone is the Enemy!

In a tense, hostile, swarming, rude-crude, stinking, multicultural, *internationale*, travellers-hostel one day :
The European said so cautiously, "'If it's not a secret', could you tell me how much you pay the manager for rent."
        The Other European cracked, "Not everyone is the enemy! ...Of course I will tell you!"
The European later asked tepidly, "Can I buy a tea-bag from you."
        The Other European laughed, "Here is one for you. Not everyone is the enemy."
The European later asked, "Some trouble with my login. If it's not a problem, could you receive the website's verification-code for me on your phone using your phone-number?"
        The Other European laughed, "Not everyone is the enemy," typing in his phone-number. "Not everyone is the enemy." ...Seeing a brief pause of no understanding in the European's face to, that oft-repeated phrase, the Other European croaked, in a flat voice, "In *war*, not everyone is the enemy. ...There are also *friends*."

---

[340] spoken whilst submitting a sacrifice into the sea to Neptune

—The European's eyes glazed over with "the light of consciousness"
 —The Other European finished his chuckle, to himself, "Not everyone is the enemy!"

Poem 155 *2022/03/19. Kraków*
Piss in a Bottle, a Dedication to Bukowsky
If I could piss in a bottle,
"It's the first thing that I'd like to do
To save time every day 'til eternity passes away"
Just to spend them with me

If I could piss in bottles forever,
"If words could make wishes come true"
I'd save time every day like a treasure, and then
Again, I would spend them with me

But there never seems to be enough piss-bottle places
"To do the things you want to do once you find them

I've looked around enough to know"
That *it's* the one I want to go through time with

If I had a bottle just for wishes,
"And dreams that had never come true"
The 'piss-bottle' would be empty
Except for the memory of how they were answered by it

But there never seems to be enough places
"To do the things you want to do once you find them

I've looked around enough to know"
That *it's* the one I want to go through time with

Poem 156 *2022/04/16. Kraków*
To Suffer the Groid
There *you* are, riding "economy,"
To suffer the groid.
The rich-man flies "first-class,"
To "avoid the groid," so saying. (Any non-European *colono*.)

There *you* are in the poor-man's group-dorm travellers-hostel,
To suffer the groid, with the tropical cough.
The rich-man sleeps in a hotel (private-room),
To "avoid the groid."

There *you* the wage-slave are living in the 6-man group-flat (of a mass-migration
overpopulated hence expensive city),

And you suffer the groid. (To save up money for *the dream* to "avoid the groid"
at-the-end-of-life.)
The salary-man owns-a-home[341] or rents a private-flat,
To "avoid the groid."

The government services offices are swarming—hate-filled *internationale* saunas. No
problema, the rich-man don't use 'em.
As population Demand grows (the curve shifts right), the *rentier* Prices rise (*and* Labour prices
lower)—"the rich get richer."
The Liberals from good-families, "the capital owning class," open borders to the swarming
non-European masses—"set the norms"—nicey-nicey,
And suffer not, the groid.

(Outro *coda*) *Oy*, ugh, *opa*.[342]
See 'em—count 'em… A one, and a two, and a three… "Sing it,"
A'watchin' th'weather …and lookin' for the signs…
   (*chorus*) to a-v-o-i-d…
        the g-r-o-i-d.

> "…from Negroid… If you encounter someone using the term 'groid,' it is important to challenge them on
> their language and explain why it is offensive. You should also report the incident to the appropriate
> authorities, such as a school administrator, website administrator, or law enforcement agency." —Google AI

Poem 157 *2022/08/01. Kraków*

Indra after Killing the Dragon [343]

> "…living beings fail to perceive their Atman. The first one to see the Atman as Brahman, asserts
> the *Upanishads*, said, '*dam adarsha*' or 'I have seen It'. Others then called this first seer as
> *Idam-dra* or 'It-seeing', which over time came to be cryptically known as 'Indra', because,
> claims *Aitareya Upanishad*, everyone including the gods like short nicknames. [folk etymology]"

Suddenly see (*véda*, video)
the world (*māyā*), things, a scene moving ;
suddenly see
things melting back by "strings" ;
suddenly see
all things come together
pulled back into a whirling summing "puller" pillar.

Pop out of nowhere
mysterious light (*Dyauspitar*)[344]
the *Agni* ignition[345]

---

[341] white-flight
[342] Ruski "oops", English ugh, Português "wow"
[343] "He who kept you back." Vritra and his "deceiving forces". Vedic root word means "resistance".
[344] "They indeed were comrades of the gods, Possessed of Truth, the poets of old: The fathers found the hidden
light And with true prayer brought forth the dawn." —*Rg-Veda*
[345] One Vedic song describes *Apam Napat* as coming out of the river, golden, and "clothed with lightning," which

that sparkling spinning (*swastika*) pillar.
At the One, the All.

Pulling thee down
swallow ("the eater") thee
gone back to the One (Brahman) [346]
dissolved into the "Indra-pole"[347] flowing. ("the world tree", dragon snake)

Arisen Manu
feel "the streams are flowing" O Indra ;
atonement (*Advaita*) to see is atonement to be ;
everything is "the way" it has to be because everything is interconnected ("net of Indra"[348])
to fit (*ar-*)[349] wholly, because all is cause-and-effect (*dharma*)[350] tree, perfectly (*ṛtá*) ;
All (the many) is perfect It has to be because It is One (*Advaita*) ;
Thee is home ;
Brahman is dwelling[351]—seeing, walking, top of the head reaching the sky (*moksha*[352]) ;
"golden-haired" hero Rudra "the wild one" goose-stepping[353] (Aryaman) ;
born-again ("twice-born") Thee redeemer (*heilbringer*) of the wasted wasteland Thee.

> "The other said: 'So it is, O Yâgñavalkya. Tell now (who is) the puller within.'
> Yâgñavalkya said: 'He who dwells in the earth, and within the earth, whom the
> earth does not know, whose body the earth is, and who pulls (rules) the earth
> within, he is thy Self, the puller (ruler) within, the immortal.'" —*Upanishads*

> "... It was always in the One. ... [...] and [...] and things on strings. Universal hole I
> see through. ..." —Charles Manson, "I'm doin' fine", song

> "Yet, in my darkest night, / And farthest drift from land, / There dawned within the
> guiding-light; / I felt the unseen hand. ... / Be theirs the victory." —Gerald Massey

Poem 158 *2022/10/20. Vilnius*

9 is the 'Blink of an Eye'

"Don't you know," you are less than one-half of one-half of 1 percent of your direct biological
grandfather 9 generations back. (Or the year *1801*.) That is to say, .025 percent of your DNA.
And usually you are actually 0 percent (not one single chromosome) of that direct ancestor 9
generations back because some DNA is lost and is not passed on over each of the generations,
recombinatory iterations.
(As an aside, don't forget, you are more than 800 percent more *general*-Neanderthal than you
are your *particular* 9th grandfather because Europeans are all 3 percent Neanderthal.

---

has been taken to mean fire.
[346] Plato's hypostasis
[347] an Aryaman/Irminsūl pole or Vedic "Indra-pole", Maypole, Yggdrasil
[348] *wyrd*
[349] *ar-*
[350] Greek *harmonia*
[351] (Heidegger's "dwelling")
[352] *psychosis*
[353] *berserkergang*

…Furthermore, statistically, in 1000 years you have had 1 billion ancestors. —2 to the power of 30. But only one Y nucleotide ; a large chromosome with 10,000 positions.)
What does this story of 9 mean? It means you are not you ; you are your group, "isn't it so."
[354] You are your gene pool—*not* your direct ancestors, *nor are you your direct descendants.*
Your DNA is your larger general racial identity (race means lineage *cours*), "do you see."
—You are your group. You "rise and fall" and you "come and go," exist or go extinct, with them, with the pool. Not with your direct descendants. 99.999 percent to 100 percent of all of your personal DNA (chromosome spelling SNPs) will disappear within 9 generations of your direct descendants. What does not disappear is the DNA group that you and your descendants' DNA is drawn from, "do you see." That alone lives on, and becomes high-culture or becomes low-culture. Unless your lineage (*raza*) group (your shared DNA, your pool) goes extinct. Like what has happened to European folks in their European homelands, "don't you know."

"Nothing is ever irreversible, except the death of a people by genocide or miscegenation." —Dom Venner

Poem 159 *2023/01/01. Esch an der Alzette*
Western Europe Scribbles : Two French-speakers
He is empty-headed and he sits with his passport-wife in silence.
Because he is empty-headed (but long of dongle).
So they peck-kiss on the lips like two chimps do and sit in silence.
Then the gracile European woman retreats to the next table and sits with her three little *mulatto* children, that share no family resemblance to her, and talks with them.
Then sits back with her big African husband in silence.

Poem 160 *2023/04/29. Kraków, Małopolska*
Hum'n 'N Hymn'n about the Caucus Sub-Humaines[355] of *Ost* Europa Hostels
> *"I don't care if it rains or freezes / Long as I got my plastic Jesus /*
> *Riding, on, the dashboard, of my car."*

Big fat hairy old Caucus men from Georgia,
Put them all in a room together.
Geezus! Hostel manager!
Keep them a-way from me-e.

They can talk a-loud together,
All-day all-night nonstop nonsense talking—like the East Europea saying, "Asiatic talk a lot."
Put them all in a room to-gather, please!
Geezus! Keep them a-way from me-e.

Taking up ter-ri-tory,
Stare 'n bark 'n push—their repute precedes them—let them bully not us any-more.
Let them Caucus fat hogs snore away all night—dimwit sub-humaines can sleep with snorers.
Geezus! Snoring away all night.

---

[354] Henry Miller
[355] "Under-man"*Untermensch* is a term created by Friedrich Nietzsche; he also used *Tschandala*

Close the door and *Ausländer raus*,
Then let in only who are us *Europer*
—*via negativa* is the way. Then I'll stay—else I'll leave.
Geezus! Please us man-a-ger!

The god-awful Caucus men, put them all in a room to-gather.
Don't make us live sub-humaine, please. Geez.
Put all proper *Europer* in a room, and put *Kavkaz* Georgian hogs out in the Other.
Ain't no Pauline equals. Geezus! Geezus! Manager, where's your "christ-consciousness" of my hu-maine-ity?
    "Through my trials and tribulations / And my travels through the nations / With my plastic Jesus I'll go far. / Plastic Jesus plastic Jesus, / Riding, on, the dashboard, of my car" (E. Marrs)
It's a nice building. —"The problem is the people."

Poem 161 *2023/10/31. Kraków, Małopolska*
Hate is True
Everything you ever thought ...was true. What you suspected.
Your hunches and gut-feelings and insula cortex *disgusts*—the hate ...was true.
All the self-serving *amigos* saying you were wrong ...were false—to you for true for them.
("The videos are wrong," with a laugh.) *So* don't "hate" is their cosmic *credo*, "licence to steal."
You *know* that now (you *saw*), the young Swede teenager told you, that "living fossil."
—*Vis-à-vis*, the truest honest foggy eyes : "Sweden is doomed...[and] can't be saved," he said,
"...the crime, unsafe... ...building highrise towers in the forests for non-European refugees."
What you saw, felt, concluded, it was true. You knew it in the long ago.
"Oh, your're one of me. You are one of me."
"Yes."
All you men who don't hate. I always say, "who taught you to love your abuser?" It wasn't me. "[Europeans] have a right to hate the people who have destroyed their lives." (Norman Finkelstein) Dispossessed men have every (moral) right to hate their dispossessors.

Poem 162 *2023/11/06. Kraków, Małopolskie*
'What Can One Man Do?'
"'Man is a wolf to Man,' dude. The Roman proverb. Or *they* were wrong and *you* are right?
You are smarter than the Roman proverb? I should believe *you* and not the Roman proverb?"
"But," you say, "'what can one man do?'"
"One man can do what *one man* can do. *That* is what one man can do.
So I do what one man can do. That is what I do. What one man can do.
I do what one man can do—I speak out.
—So to one brother who says something right, I say, 'yeah man you're right about that.' And to an other indoctrinated brother who says something wrong, I say, 'game theoretically, you're wrong about that universalistic individualism economic ideology, deluded.'
Because I care. I do it because I care.

That is what one man can do. And that is what I'm doing.

That is why we speak to you. Because we care."

Blank-faced, no response, *of course*.

Poem 163 *2023/11/11. Kraków, Małopolska,* counter-currents.com/2023/11/whats-the-matter-with-social-metaphysics

To the Authoritarian Personalities (Or, Yet Another Allegory of 'The Allegory of the Cave')

You will not believe what I say. You will not believe what I tell you because you *cannot* believe what I say. You can't.

You cannot believe what I say because you have an authoritarian personality.

People with an "authoritarian personality" means simply that they only believe "authority figures." They are *social*. (—Everyone is authoritarian. You, me, everyone. We all are.)

So you can't believe me. Because I am not an authority figure.

You only believe totalising (capitalist) billionaires and the elites and the dom mainstream-media norms of what is morally up good and down bad. The Hegemony.

If I was an authority figure and told you "what is what," on a leading figure Public domain platforming, and possessed some consensus of space, then you would not cannot-believe me.

But you cannot believe me because you are authoritarian.

To believe me would require partisan perspective ("a backbone"), particular (quantitative) logic, and particular (critical) study.

As an universalistic authoritarian, you can't. Or, you can't, so you are authoritarian.

Too bad, boo-hoo. Taboo for you!

> "Man is born free, and everywhere he is in chains." —Rousseau

> "All sheep are born carnivores, and everywhere they eat grass." —Conor Cruise O'Brien

Poem 164 *2024/02/16. Kraków, Małopolska*

Midnight Conjectures

> "Alongside this tradition of 'perennial philosophy' is the perennial mystical tradition, the common core of which is the individual's experience of his identity with the hidden one. 'All' are identical with the 'one,' but only the few directly *experience* this identity." —Greg Johnson

> *In my midnight conjectures / When I think all the things that I want to!*

We have two selves. *Manu*[356] and *Yemo*.[357]

> *La-la da / La-la, da, da-da, da, da!*

Our individual *ego*—our particular self—that we see and know and feel and experience and hear—the front cortex perhaps.

And behind that is an invisible hidden over-soul (*Paramātman*), "the One" of Neo-Platonism, Brahman—that you don't see and don't know ; an *axis mundi* in the mind, for a "ground of being" feeling of "embedded Aspect".

Looping betwixt the *duo* (the particular and the universal)—the self and the Self—allows for Hofstedler's "strange loop" theory of consciousness, perhaps. A looping so there can be consciousness experienced, perhaps. The design trick happed upon by evolutionary process. To

---

[356] "Man", the sacrificer, who uses the body of his twin to create the world.

[357] "Twin", the sacrificed primordial being, whose dismembered body becomes the cosmos.

render a *simulacrum* feel of consciousness to hold cognisance. Not just the unknowingness of other beasts.

La-la da / La-la, da, da-da, da, da!
In my midnight conjectures / When I think all the things that I want to!

"Predication in philosophy refers to an act of judgement where one term is subsumed under another. A comprehensive conceptualization describes it as the understanding of the relation expressed by a predicative structure primordially (*i.e.* both originally and primarily) through the opposition between particular and general or the one and the many." —Wikipedia

"the one" (Schopenhauer's "*Wille*") / "the many" (Schopenhauer's "representation")

Poem 165 *2024/10/5. Puerto Villarta, Mexico*

Args [358]

Everything isn't words. Everything is arguments.[359] (AI's "tokens".)[360]

That chair is an argument and that bottle is an argument and that light is an argument ; everything in this room is an argument. All objects are arguments.

Just as vectors are functions which can also be args ; and scalars are args. …And tuple elements within a set.

The mathematicians taught us that. Arguments are what goes into math equations. The mathematicians call them "args". And arguments are the name for what is "passed" into a programmer's functions (linguistics' predicates), running this phone.[361] "It from bit." [362]

And in Aristotelian Logic, each statement in the *argument* is called a "premise," and the final statement is the "conclusion".

And an author's words.

All real grounded-objects and fictional imaginary ungrounded-objects are arguments. Plus non-linguistic thoughts are arguments.

All the billboard signs and advertising and brands and words and ideas and function concepts and statements are arguments. And you and mine are arguments. And sights in dreams are args.

And words and phonemes and tagmemes and syntaxes are arguments.

And physical ions[363] going through synapses. Both arguments.

And protein coded chromosomes.

Now let predicate *my* morals and *values* and politics and selling and articles and yield up out

---

[358] The concept of arguments as inputs to functions arose during the development of Calculus, 17th century. Leibniz and Newton worked with functions that took different input values and produced corresponding output values. "Argument" chosen to emphasise the idea that the input value was being "argued" or presented to the function as a **parameter**.
In logic and proofs, "argument" derives from its use in rhetoric and philosophy. In these fields, arguments are used to persuade others of a particular point of view. The adoption of "argument" in mathematics was influenced by the idea that mathematical proofs are a form of logical argumentation.
[359] Concepts/functions are "extensions" (sets of sets), says Frege. So functions are also objects/arguments (of sets)!
[360] The analogy holds in a very high-level conceptual sense: Input Data: Both tokens and args are the values or data provided *to* a processing unit (an LLM or a function) to get an output.
[361] "arguments" are the values that are *input* into the function to produce an *output*.
[362] "bit" is Claude Shannon's *portemanteau* of "binary-digit".
[363] a 3 atom molecule

over to me my argument.[364]

Schopenhauer called *die Wille* (Vedic's "Self") "the womb of *die Welt*."

> Frege provides a definition of the distinction between function and argument: "If, in an expression (whose content need not be assertible), a simple or a complex symbol occurs in one or more places and we imagine it as replaceable by another (but the same one each time) at all or some of these places, then we call the part of the expression that shows itself invariant a function and the replaceable part its argument." [Frege, *1879*]

Poem 166   *2024/12/25. Bratislava*

Way More Evil

Everything you see in your *Welt* is your Representation (*Vorstellung*).[365] The World you see is your Will's Representation, says Schopenhauer's book, like the *Upanishads* called it (Will) the Self. All your loves are "for the sake of the Self," the piece of the Absolute inside your mind, said the *varna* brahmin *Arier* in Sanskrit more than two millennia agone.

Yeah, the *Wille*, or "the womb of the world," Schopenhauer phrased it. The Brahman of the *Upanishads* to Plotinus's "One"[366] are described as the source of all existence (*Dasein*), all being, all particulars, all *māyā*.[367]

So, if that be so, whatever *you* think is evil,

> Is *way more* evil,
>> Because it's *you*.

Full stop. …Full circle.

"[We] are already dead [anyway]. (Krishna)" Hence, counter intuitively, the message *is*, do evil to your enemies, to prevent evil being done to you'uns, counselled the *Bhagavad-Gita*'s Krishna-soul charioteer to Arjuna.

> "Time am I. Time, the mighty destroyer, am I. Doomed they are. Whether you fight or not, *they are already dead.* Even without you, your foes will escape no death. Arise, O Arjuna, arise! Victory's glory and renown you win. Conquer your enemies." —*Bhagavad-Gita*, Krishna's argument for a justified war. This is the section that Oppenheimer quoted that says "Now I [Krishna] am become Death the destroyer of worlds" that Oppenheimer used to justify his Jewish team's creation of the Atomic bomb meant to be dropped on *their* German ("Aryan") enemies ("*not* the Japanese"), as he is recorded to have protested to President Truman.

Poem 167   *2025/1/29. Kraków*

Traveller in Time

Hey, so you're interested in "time travel," in Physics. You're always talking about time travel. Well, there is an other sort of time travel, that is not out there, in *universal* level Physics. It's a relative sort of time travel—at a *particular* level. When two different timeline subjectivities meet—two particular men from different ages.

Check it :

---

[364] "motivated reasoning"

[365] The opening sentence of Schopenhauer's work is *Die Welt ist meine Vorstellung*: "the world is my representation" (alternatively, "idea" or "presentation").

[366] "the supreme identity"

[367] Sanskrit "appearance"

So you have a timeline ; as of now yours is 25 years old long.

And I have one ; I am 50, so my timeline is twice as long as yours ; relative to yours where you are at ; right now.

Where I am at right now on my line, is in the future from where you are at right now on your line. But yet I am meeting and talking to you here right now, at this kitchen-counter.

I am from the future, relative, to your particular timeline, right now.

So I am talking to you from the future, right now.

25 years from now you will be at where my timeline, from my age, is at right now.

I was where you are at now, in your age, 25 years before you came. But here I am speaking to you now at this hostel kitchen-counter, while you are supping some vittles.

So I am talking to you from the future right now. That's time travel, but not universal level Physics time travel.

I am travelling back in time, to talk to your timeline, right now, as we speak, *vis-à-vis*.

But it doesn't do any good to time travel, because your age can't believe me, if I tell you about the future, which is where I'm from, relative to you. You can't believe me, because I am not an "authority figure," to you, at your age. Men can only believe authority figures (because we all have an "authoritarian personality"). I'm not an authority figure ; so time travel doesn't work.

Traveller in time / You'll see / Wait for your destiny

Some rare, "low time preference" farsighted traveller in time, perhaps, could, sometime, over the horizon line see, what I tell about "what's what" from at the future.

"Like what?"

As a snowball rolls down a hill, it grows exponentially—"the snowball effect," compounding. Each year is one revolution, one layer of snow on the ball, the bigger the ball, the more surface area of snow, with each rotation. The higher the hill the bigger the snowball becomes, in the end.

"The hill is Time."

Yes! And there will never be a higher starting point on the hill than today. (And it only is well effective from one particular lifetime's *one-time* highest hill.)

So a man shouldn't go to uni for 5 years. That priceless age, 18, at the top of the hill, the well highest hill. He should make french-fries at MacDonald's full-time (or more) for those 5 years (then he can stop, at 24) and save every dollar and plant it *all* into an index-fund and then not ever buy or sell it (because Bachelier's phrase "The mathematical expectation of the speculator is zero"). At 50 it (just those 5 years of earnings) will be a million[368] *fortuna* ; so you won't need to be a life-long wage-slave, in prison "working for the man."

But no lad your age ever does what I say. *Das kapitalistische Hegemonie* high-social-status or rich or institutional authority figures inform him to go to "uni" at that precious Time ; with his Christian-American circumcised up dick that he doesn't even know that he has.

Traveller in time / You'll see / Wait for your destiny

"They needs must find it hard to take Truth for authority who have so long mistaken Authority for truth." —Goethe

---

[368] The final amount after compounding $200,000 at 6% annual return for 30 years is $1,148,698.23.

"Every gold piece you save is a slave to work for you." —Clason, *Richest Man in Babylon*

"Unbecoming to a gentleman, too, and vulgar are the means of livelihood of all hired workmen whom we pay for mere manual labour [*negotium*], not for artistic skill; for in their case the **very wage** they receive is a **pledge of their slavery**." —Cicero

Poem 168 *2025/8/18. Lviv*

An Address to Nietzsche's "The White Race of 'Liberals' of Every Age" [369]

Difference is identity. —The particular—quantification.

The concept that *information* is differences is a well-established idea. Claude Shannon and Bateson defined information as a "difference that makes a difference." —The definition of information is differences ; sameness means no information. (And why didn't you know that? Who led you otherwise?)

Differences are negations (Leibniz's and Spinoza's *via negativa* of the undifferentiated One). Like the word critical.

G. W. F. Hegel taught the thought that the important events in History, to study and know about History, are the "negatives" or the "slaughter-bench of history" driven by the "cunning of reason."[370]

Telling me your positive opinions "tells me nothing." You spineless worm, tell me the negatives, god damn it! All I want is the negatives.

I always see You are always so *shy* to say. You are a free man! You can say whatever You want. There is not an eye in the sky watching You.

Liberals—driven by universalism—Pauline equality—sameness—anti-different—enemy denial—are *not* interesting. "There's the rub."

Did You think I didn't know You? Did You think I didn't know who You are? Did You think I hadn't met You *countless times*?

I have met you ten-thousand times.

You done good. Now go back to work, and smile. You won't lose Your job.

Poem 169 *2025/10/9. Kraków*

The Heġemony is Inside You

"Do you want to tar-and-feather them?"

Huh, why did you say that, that's a strange thing to think. Why would I want to do that? Where did you get the idea to say that? Where did you get that thought? Why did you say *that*?

"I don't know. Nowhere."

I don't want to do anything to anyone.

That thought must have come from somewhere. Else you wouldn't have said it. Why would I do that?

"I don't know I just said it."

But why did you say *that*? Where did it come from? Where did you get that idea?

---

[369] philosophy.ucsc.edu/news-events/colloquia-conferences/GeneologyofMorals.pdf
[370] Karl Marx concluded that violence is the only effective force in history.

"I don't know. It didn't come from anywhere."
No, it came from somewhere.
"No."
Yes it did.
"No it didn't."
Everything comes from somewhere.
[flat monotone] The heġemony. It's the heġemony. The heġemony is inside you.
[speechless] ▌

hen to pan (ἓν τὸ πᾶν), "the All is One"

"No. Caesar still weak. Ape only follow strong." [371]
—*Planet of the Apes,* newer movie

[371] wikipedia.org/wiki/Social_learning_theory ceacb.ucl.ac.uk/cultureclub/files/2004-2005/CC2004-11-25-Henrich%20and%20Gil-White2001.pdf

Finis | *Ende*

snore

Not a human ape and not a chimp ape. A baboon monkey.

Afterword

 372

2012/4/2.

Horus's Sacrifice of His Eye[373] for His Father Osiris

DRAMATIS PERSONÆ

Man
Christian girl
Spirits *krestos*[374] Horus & his Father Osiris[375] *presented by* Christ Jesus & his Father
Attendants

ACT I

Scene I.   [*America. A public setting.*]
Bright fluorescent-lit public room with college students working and chatting and sitting at individual computer-tables.
Seated is a man. [Man]
Enter a nineteen-year old baby-voiced blanco girl. [Christian girl].

"We have to remember that *doing* was earlier than *saying*, and the
dumb drama was acted first." —Massey, on Egyptian religion.

Christian girl. "Hi."
Man. [*celebratory smiling*] "Hi-i."
Christian girl. "How are you?"
Man. [*celebratory smiling*] "How are you-u?" [*laughing open mouth smile*]
(They knew each other.)
Christian girl. "Can I ask you a strange question?"
Man. "Yes." [*smile*]
Christian girl. "Are you a Chr-istian?"

---

[372] the "eye of Horus"
[373] "The figure of an eye directly represents sight and seeing, " (Massey)
[374] Means the "resurrected" Horus
[375] Harpin, *The Pagan Christ,* Krestos was an Egyptian term for the resurrecting Horus. Discovered by Gerald Massey, *The Natural Genesis.*

Man. "[*forced*] I'm not going to lie to you."

Christian girl. "[*sigh, pout*] You shouldn't hav-vv to-oo."

Man. "[*strained, quick*] I-ee-don't-have-a-religious-personality."

Christian girl. "That's okay-y."

Man. [*stunned, shocked, speechless gaze.*]

Christian girl. "[*gaze*] You don't neee-ed to have a religious personality."

Man. [*stunned, speechless gaze.*]

Christian girl. "[*gaze*] You don't nee-ed to have religious personaliiity-y"

Man. [*Stunned speechless gaze. Eyes bulge and glaze over.*]

Christian girl. "[*gaze, pout.*] You don't need to have a religious personality."

Man. [*paralyzed. popping eye.*]

Christian girl. "[*gaze*] ...You don't need to have a religious personality....to be a Christian."

Man. "[*snaps to.*] Oh, well[376], that's not something that I think about."

Christian girl. "Why not?"

Man. [*gaze*] "I don't think about it."[377]

Christian girl. "Why?"

Man. "I don't think about that."

Christian girl. "Why not?"

Man. "That's not something that I think about."

Christian girl. "Why don't you think about it."

Man. "I just don't think about it."

Christian girl. "Why not?"

Man. "That's just not something that I think about all the time."

Christian girl. "[*sigh*] Oh."

Christian girl. "... Do you believe in the Resurrection?"

Man. [*Aside : The Man's own voice, in third-person, speaks loud and clearly in his mind (momentarily lights dimmed, light on him, turning to the audience), "She's trying to get you to lie to her." (Spoken by Attendant)*]

Man. "[*gaze*] When I was young I used to ask what-if questions. I don't think it's about logic."

Christian girl. "[*sigh. spoken with feeling*] Yeah."

Man. "You ask me a lot of personal questions."

Christian girl. [*quickly*] "I'm sor-ry"

Man. [—*before she can finish; eyes totally wide-round and poking out—like a parent to a baby—high, throaty feeling*] "No-o-o, I like it." [*smiling, laughing*]

Christian girl. [*smiling-eyes narrowing*]

Christian girl. [*imploringly, forelornsom-ly*] "... Why aren't you a Christian?"

Man. [*Aside: The man's thought, in third-person, sees clearly in his mind (momentarily lights dimmed, light on him, turning to the audience), "Don't out." (spoken by Attendant)*]

Man. "[*sorrowful sigh with eyebrows crooking up at the center, then... serious, accusatorily*] "Why should I explain it."

---

[376] etymology: weal, wealth

[377] "Kant famously denied that the cognitive unification of particulars that occurs in thought—say the unification of two events in a judgement about causal connection—can be explained empirically." Michael S. Green

Christian girl. "Oh."

Man. "... [*gaze*] Is your father a born-again Christian?"

Christian girl. "No."

Man. "Well *you* should ask him. He can explain it to you better than I can."

Christian girl. "Oh."

Christian girl. "... Why did you ask me if my father was a born-again Christian?"

Man. "Well, some other people asked me why I was not a Christian. And I told them they should ask their father."

"He can explain it to them better than I can."

"... [*Gaze. Briefly, a* Ra[378] *'pagan sun-halo' flat circular placard-board held behind his head by Attendant stagehand with a long wooden-pole, a quick brief burst of vaudeville angelic harp-music that stops, and placard removed*] You've known your father your whole life."

"He can explain it to you better than I can—You've known your *Father*[379] your whole life." [*with feeling*] "...Your *whole* life."

Christian girl. "Oh-h." [*disappointed pout*]

Man. "[*sad sigh. feelingly*] ...I like your bible-group. When I go to other bible-groups. The men come-on to me. They tell me to get down on my knees and submit to them. [*glazed gaze past her*] That's too [*lip snarl*] aggressive."

Christian girl. "Oh-hh."

Exchange of pleasantries.
Man *sits in a celebratory mood.*

Exit the Christian girl, *nonplussed.*

Exeunt.

"But under the second root [of the ash tree Yggdrasil, the world tree], which extends to the frost-giants, is the well of Mimer [memory], wherein knowledge and wisdom are concealed. The owner of the well hight Mimer. He is full of wisdom, for he drinks from the well with the Gjallar-horn [grail]. Alfather [Odin] once came there and asked for a drink from the well, but he did not get it before he layed [plucked out] one of his eyes as a pledge. .... So it is said in the Vala's Prophecy: Well know I, Odin, Where you hid your eye: In the crystal-clear Well of Mimer." —Snorre's *Edda*

---

[378] "Amen-Ra, the *Hidden* Sun ..." (Massey)

[379] "... Horus, the 'son of Osiris,' is explained to be '*the sun himself.*'" (Massey)

[stub]

2024-01-10
♀ Kraków

Appendix

"It is particularly amusing to hear through the mouth of 'God's chosen' people, that incontrovertible racial and species solidarity is considered anti-semitism …. The very principle of Zionism [and Jew, Jewish, and Judaism] is built on the racial solidarity of the Jews." —book

"For if there is no such thing as the resurrection of the dead, then Christ was never raised. And if Christ was not raised then neither our preaching nor your faith has any meaning at all. Further it would mean that we are lying in our witness for God, for we have given our solemn testimony that he did raise up Christ—and that is utterly false if it should be true that the dead do not, in fact, rise again! For if the dead do not rise neither did Christ rise, and if Christ did not rise your faith is futile and your sins have never been forgiven. Moreover those who have died believing in Christ are utterly dead and gone. Truly, if our hope in Christ were limited to this life only we should, of all mankind be the most to be pitied!" —Paul (founder of Christianity for *goyim*)

"In actual operation Nature is cruel and merciless to men, as to all other beings. Let a tribe of human animals live a rational life, Nature will smile upon them and their posterity; but let them attempt to organise an unnatural mode of existence an equality elysium, and they will be punished even to the point of extermination." —Ragnar Redbeard
".., for belief in one false principle, is the beginning of all unwisdom." —Redbeard
"...Pythagoras dedicated entire tracts to the given question, and for his part, Plato wrote that in devoting high honours to the Olympian Gods—'everything odd, first, and right' was required; and to the Gods of the Underworld went 'everything even, secondary, and left.'" —Redbeard

"shared bits = semantic similarity" — L. Susskind

As Cantor showed, some infinities are bigger than other infinities; that is why the hare beats the tortoise (Zeno's paradox). —para. a mathematician

"Hobbes says thought is syntactic manipulation of basic atomic units."

linguistic universal: Lakoff showed that linguistic metaphors may be common to most languages because they are based on general human experience, for example, metaphors likening *up* with good and bad with *down*.

"There is a superposition between you two. How should I collapse it?" —quipped the host of a discussion-panel of physicists talking, where two panellists disagreed about what to do next.

~~Punctuation.~~
~~Breath it in—we think in lengths of breath—we talk in lengths of breath.~~
~~And we write in lengths of breath. —Sentence to a period.~~
~~We poem in lines, metres, to a breath (*prana*).~~

Glossary

sentential: a sentence, a proposition. | **sentience:** feeling, qualia.
stochastic: random chance. (*hap, luck*)
Heuristic: wikipedia.org/wiki/Heuristic
bayesian: "rule to be derived from the axioms of probability theory is Bayes' Theorem, which tells you exactly how your probability for a statement should change as you encounter new information. ... If you're not using Bayes' Theorem to update your beliefs, then you're violating probability theory, which is an extension of logic. ...
... a quick explanation of why frequentism, the theory of probability you probably learned in school..., is wrong. Whereas the Bayesian view sees probability as a measure of uncertainty about the world, frequentism sees probability as "the proportion of times the event would occur in a long run of repeated experiments."
data point: a datum. wikipedia.org/wiki/Data_point. aka a vector: **vectors** may be added together and multiplied ("scaled") by real numbers, called *scalars*.
disjunction: either, or.
conjunction: and. (copulative conjunction: grammarist.com/grammar/conjunctions)
function word: wikipedia.org/wiki/**Function_word** (wikipedia.org/wiki/Grammaticalization)
a theorem in logic: "From a contradiction you can deduce everything."
Pāṇini **rules:** for example, focus of the 'negative prefix' **in-**: if an n̲ is immediately followed by a consonant pronounced with the lips, like b̲, change the n̲ to m̲.

"In general, the **dative** marks the indirect object of a verb, although in some instances the dative is used for the direct object of a verb pertaining directly to an act of giving something."

Some S are not P. —In **predicate logic**: $(\exists_x)(S_x \cdot \sim P_x)$ ...['$(\exists_x)$' is an **existential quantifier** saying that there is an x in the universe and that x DOES exist.]
equivalency: means "if-and-only-if" which means "the same as". ($\equiv$)
more logic symbols: $\int$ $\therefore$ $::$ $\supset$ $\exists_x$ $\cdot$ $\sim$ $\wedge$ ... **universal quantifier**: "$\forall(x)$"
"::" means 'logically equivalent'. wikipedia.org/wiki/List_of_logic_symbols
AND is sometimes called Logical Product "$\cdot$". OR is called the Logical Sum ("+")

Neo-Gramscianism: wikipedia.org/wiki/Neo-Gramscianism
binary opposition: wikipedia.org/wiki/Binary_opposition
Framing Effect: wikipedia.org/wiki/Framing_effect_(psychology)
empty signifier: wikipedia.org/wiki/Floating_signifier
status function, deontic power, speech act: newrepublic.com/book/review/whatever-you-say
Group Evolutionary Strategy:
Group Selection: YouTube.com/watch?v=dEaMtSLwkDs   YouTube.com/watch?v=INJ4rKXXmwo
Social Cheating: wikipedia.org/wiki/Cheating_(biology)

Bibliography / References

Rosenfels, Paul *Love And Power*. San Francisco: Random House, 1970. Electronic, Pdf.

E., E. E. *Game Theory: Everyday Applications*, 2020. <http://programmabilities.com/p/game-theory-everyday-applications.html>

E., E. E. *The Marxist Analysis of Immigration*, 2019. <http://programmabilities.com/p/the-marxist-analysis-of-immigration.html>

E., E. E. *A Warm Mirror Neuron On A Memory*, 2016. <http://programmabilities.com/p/warm-mirror-neuron-on-memory.html>

Ibid. T.H.B., 1995. <http://programmabilities.com/p/thb.html>

MacDonald, Kevin B. *Culture Of Critique*. San Francisco: Random House, 2002. Electronic, Pdf.

Nietzsche, Friedrich *Towards a Genealogy of Morals*. Basel: Random House, 1882. Electronic, Pdf.

Transgenic

Index Register

Author's Bio

E.E.E. "was born to a [non-]Jewish family." The author has the relation of a Leftist who is defending an in-group. Speaking as a #ethnicEuropean, she/he/they/We/it is a Frankfurt School Marxist[380] (a postmodernist *ergo* Heideggerian and Schmittian)—an *Europäisch-Identität* partisan[381]; both a Lëtzebuerger European and an American European[382] (dual passports); a

Descendant of Roger Williams second-generation "*Grand Replacement*[383] survivor" now living refugeedom in "*solidarna* Polska."[384] A woke "social justice warrior"[385] for European identified menfolk. Holding degrees of AASc computer programming and BSc economics—a programmer by profession and a *rentier*[386] by trade. With a Ukraïner[387] [388] Defense Department ATO combat zone press-card—present the day 100 civilians were murdered on Maidan square by the Muscovy ("*Moskal*") horde's[389] snipers; as Putin liberated Ukraïner from "fascism" and "de-nazified" Ukraine like back in Nuremburg trials times. The stylist of this textuality is a pro-gay, a pagan, a collectivist, an anti-capitalist, an anti-dispossession activist, a researcher in anti-European studies (Holodomor Outreach Program), pro-tolerance of European in-groups, and an environmentalist (population-control). Confronting anti-Europeanism and defending rights of *Europäer* bodies worldwide. —A watchdog of defamation and hate. Teaching European identitarians to pledge to work together to combat hate—to combat the *blancocide* project. Review at Goodreads.com/programmabilities.

> *"Mir wëlle bleiwe wat mir sinn.* [translate]*"* —national *motto* of Lëtzebuerger folk

---

[380] "cultural marxism" *for* white-people *via* intolerance; identity-politics and you are likely to use bias (compression algorithms) on the relatively interpreted world,.

[381] "Schmitt's hope is that globalisation and homogenization will not be completed because they will give rise to partisans who will resist the process in the name of their own particularity: their distinct homelands, cultures, and ways of life." (Greg Johnson)

[382] "To begin with, the Jews are unquestionably a race, not a religious community. The Jew himself never describes himself as a Jewish Deutsche, a Jewish Polski or a Jewish American, but always as a Deutsche, Polski, or American Jew." (hitler.org/writings/first_writing)

[383] un.org/en/development/desa/population/publications/ageing/Replacement-migration.asp

[384] ("united Poland")

[385] Hegel coined "social justice".

[386] usury: dividend-collector / rent-collector / money-lender.

[387] "The Pale of the Settlement"

[388] (Formerly Lemberg Österreich, then ethnically cleansed of Deutsche, and then formerly Lwów Polska, then ethnically-cleansed of *Polakiem*.)

[389] horde: from the word *urdu*—the Tatar Yoke

Review / Contact: Goodreads.com/programmabilities
Published by Programmabilities.com®

About this book:
An *avant-garde* book of modern poetry. Some "random thoughts"—some poems about thoughts and about moods and about grammars about European-identified man. "Recollections of the mind—catch yourself thinking." (Allen Ginsberg)

amazon.com/*Warm-Mirror-Neuron-Memory*-ebook/dp/B00GQFT6QM/?tag=programmabi0e-20

ISBN 978-1-7326264-2-3 (electronic)
ISBN 978-0-615-56694-8 (paper)

ISBN 978-0-615-56694-8
50015
9 780615 566948

For sale:
- **Amazon**.com/dp/B00GQFT6QM
- books.**Google**.com/books?vid=ISBN9780615566948
- books2read.com/programmabilities